The Tech Savvy Bride

Using AI to Master Wedding Planning

Published By: Whyle's Publishing House

Alicia Hernandez-Whyle

The Tech Savvy Bride

Copyright © 2024 by Alicia Hernandez-Whyle

All rights reserved.

No part of this publication may be reproduced in any form or by any electronic or mechanical means, including information storage and retrieval systems, without written permission from the author, except for the use of brief quotations in a book review.

ISBN 978-2-5524-3454-0

Alicia Hernandez-Whyle

The Tech Savvy Bride

Introduction 8

Part One: Getting Started 11

Chapter One 12

Understanding AI and Its Role in Wedding Planning 12

Chapter Two 26

Setting Up Your Digital Planning Toolbox 26

Part Two: Planning with Precision 47

Chapter Three 48

Budgeting: Keeping Costs Under Control 48

Chapter Four 65

Venue Selection: Finding the Perfect Spot 65

Chapter Five 90

Streamlining Vendor Coordination with AI 90

Part Three: Design and Personalization 105

Chapter Six 106

Food and Menu Planning with AI 106

Chapter Seven 125

Curating Your Wedding Style with AI 125

Chapter Eight 136

Dress to Impress: AI in Bridal Fashion 136

Chapter Nine 155

Invitations and Guest Management with AI 155

Part Four: The Big Day.. 169

Chapter Ten.. 170

Ceremony Coordination 170

Chapter Eleven... 189

Wedding Day Logistics: Staying on Track 189

Chapter Twelve 208

Photography and Videography: Capturing Memories with AI..208

Chapter Thirteen 225

Entertainment and Music: Creating the Perfect Ambience........225

Chapter Fourteen... 243

AI for Legal and Administrative Tasks.................................... 243

Part Five: After the Wedding.. 250

Chapter Fifteen.. 251

Post-Wedding Bliss: Preserving and Sharing Memories............251

Part Six: Real-Life Stories and Case Studies............................ 263

Chapter Sixteen 264

Success Stories: Brides Who Mastered AI in Wedding Planning
....264

Appendix 286

About the Author 309

Also By Alicia Hernandez-Whyle 311

Alicia Hernandez-Whyle

Introduction

Welcome to "The Tech-Savvy Bride: Using AI to Master Wedding Planning," where we embark on a journey through the evolving era of wedding planning, exploring how technology and artificial intelligence (AI) have transformed this cherished tradition.

Wedding planning, once a simple affair deeply rooted in tradition, has undergone a remarkable shift in the modern world. Gone are the days of handwritten invitations and local customs guiding every decision. Instead, today's couples navigate the intricate world of wedding planning armed with an arsenal of digital tools and technological marvels that promise convenience, creativity, and unique personalization.

In this book, we will delve into the historical perspective of wedding planning, tracing its roots back to community-centered celebrations where families and friends played important roles in organizing and executing the event. Here we will contrast this with modern approaches, highlighting how technology has transformed the planning process. Today, tools such as online platforms, apps, and AI-powered assistants streamline tasks, making it easier for couples to plan their special day. We'll explore how these innovations have shifted the responsibilities from large groups to more individualized planning, offering convenience and customization like never before.

But it's not just about convenience; it's about creativity too. The internet serves as an endless well of inspiration, from whimsical fairytale affairs to sleek, minimalist chic. Social media platforms fuel this creative explosion, offering countless ideas and facilitating seamless communication with wedding professionals.

Moreover, technology has enhanced accessibility, ensuring that guests who cannot attend in person can still be part of the celebration through live streaming services and virtual reality technologies. And for guests with disabilities, features like closed captioning and digital signage ensure a dignified and inclusive experience.

Also, we will explore how the integration of AI further revolutionizes the field of wedding planning, offering innovative solutions and enhancing the journey to the big day. From streamlined planning processes to unleashing creativity and bridging the traditional with the methods.

Join us as we examine the journey from traditional to tech-savvy wedding planning and discover how today's brides can blend the best of both worlds to create an unforgettable celebration.

Whether you're a tech-savvy bride, a groom with a passion for innovation, or a wedding professional embracing the digital age, this book is your guide to mastering wedding planning in the era of AI and technology.

Part One: Getting Started

Alicia Hernandez-Whyle

Chapter One

Understanding AI and Its Role in Wedding Planning

In the digital age, artificial intelligence (AI) has become a transformative force across various industries, and wedding planning is no exception. This chapter examines the intricate world of AI and its transformative effect on wedding planning.

Artificial intelligence (AI) technologies are transforming wedding preparation by streamlining tasks and enhancing personalization, making the journey to the big day more efficient and tailored for couples. We will explore AI's integration into different aspects of wedding planning, from budget management and vendor selection to guest interaction and beyond. Understanding AI's role in wedding planning is about embracing technological advancements and leveraging them to create unforgettable experiences that reflect the unique personalities and preferences of the couple.

Let us explore the captivating fusion of love, technology, and innovation in wedding planning. To begin, we need to understand the fundamentals of AI and machine learning and their roles in transforming this industry.

Understanding AI and Machine Learning

Before we dive deeper into the specific applications of AI in wedding planning, it's important to understand the foundational concepts of AI and machine learning. These basic terms will equip you with the knowledge needed to make the most of AI tools and technologies.

Artificial Intelligence (AI): This refers to creating computer systems capable of performing tasks that usually require human intelligence. These tasks encompass understanding natural language, recognizing patterns, learning from experience, and making decisions. AI's goal is to mimic human cognitive functions in machines.

Example: In wedding planning, AI can assist you by understanding your preferences through conversations, recognizing patterns in your choices, learning from your feedback, and making personalized recommendations.

Machine Learning: A subset of AI, machine learning focuses on empowering machines to learn from data without explicit programming. Instead of relying on predefined rules, machine learning algorithms analyze large datasets to identify patterns and make predictions or decisions. It's like teaching a computer to learn from examples rather than giving it step-by-step instructions.

Example: Machine learning can analyze data from hundreds of weddings to help you predict trends, such as the most popular flower arrangements for your chosen season, or suggest the best catering options based on your budget and dietary preferences.

With a solid understanding of AI and machine learning, we can now explore how these advanced technologies are revolutionizing wedding planning.

How AI is Revolutionizing Wedding Planning

AI offers numerous benefits that can make the planning process more efficient, personalized, and cost-effective.

Automated Task Management: AI-powered platforms and tools automate various tasks involved in wedding planning, such as scheduling appointments, sending reminders, and managing vendor communications. This automation saves time and reduces the administrative burden on couples and planners, allowing them to focus on more creative and meaningful aspects of the wedding.

Data Analysis and Insights: AI algorithms can analyze vast amounts of data to provide valuable insights into trends, preferences, and budget optimization. By analyzing historical data and user preferences, AI can recommend venues, vendors, and decor options tailored to the couple's unique tastes, ultimately enhancing the overall wedding experience.

Personalized Recommendations: AI-driven recommendation systems can suggest personalized wedding elements based on individual preferences, cultural backgrounds, and budget constraints. Whether it's recommending the perfect venue, floral arrangements, or catering options, AI ensures that every aspect of the wedding reflects the couple's vision and style.

Enhanced Guest Experience: AI-powered chatbots and virtual assistants can provide instant assistance to wedding guests, addressing their inquiries about the event schedule, directions, accommodations, and more. These virtual concierge services enhance the guest experience by providing timely and personalized support, leading to higher guest satisfaction levels.

Predictive Planning and Risk Management: AI algorithms can predict potential issues or bottlenecks in the wedding planning process, allowing couples and planners to proactively address them before they escalate. From predicting weather conditions to anticipating traffic delays, AI helps mitigate risks and ensure a seamless execution of the event.

Cost Optimization: AI-driven tools can optimize wedding budgets by analyzing pricing trends, negotiating vendor contracts, and identifying cost-saving opportunities without compromising quality. By maximizing the value of every dollar spent, AI helps couples achieve their dream wedding within their budget constraints.

As we can see, AI is transforming traditional wedding planning by streamlining processes, enhancing personalization, and optimizing costs. These advancements empower couples to create unforgettable and stress-free celebrations of love.

Debunking Myths About AI in Wedding Planning

Despite the clear benefits, some common misconceptions about AI in wedding planning may cause hesitation. Let's address these myths and provide clarity on the realities.

Loss of Personal Touch:

Myth: There's a prevailing fear that integrating AI into wedding planning will strip away the personal touch and human connection traditionally associated with such a deeply emotional event.

Reality: Contrary to this belief, AI serves as a catalyst for enhancing the personalization of weddings. While AI streamlines certain logistical aspects, it does so in a manner that complements rather than replaces human involvement. Couples retain full control over the creative direction of their wedding, with AI acting as a supportive tool to actualize their vision. By leveraging AI's analytical capabilities, couples can curate a celebration that authentically reflects their unique love story, ensuring that every detail resonates with sentimental significance.

Alicia Hernandez-Whyle

One-Size-Fits-All Solutions:

Myth: There's a misconception that AI-driven wedding planning solutions offer generic recommendations that fail to capture the individuality of each couple.

Reality: AI thrives on personalization, harnessing data insights to tailor recommendations to the specific preferences and cultural nuances of each couple. By analyzing vast datasets, AI algorithms discern nuanced patterns and trends, allowing for highly customized suggestions across various aspects of wedding planning. From venue selections to thematic inspirations, AI empowers couples to infuse their wedding with distinctive elements that reflect their personalities and aspirations, thereby transcending cookie-cutter approaches and ensuring an unparalleled experience for all involved.

Security and Privacy Concerns:

Myth: Concerns abound regarding the security and privacy implications of entrusting sensitive wedding-related data to AI-powered platforms.

Reality: Reputable AI providers prioritize the safeguarding of data privacy and security. Through robust encryption measures and adherence to stringent data protection regulations, AI platforms ensure that confidential information remains shielded from unauthorized access or misuse. By partnering with trusted AI vendors and exercising due diligence in data management practices, couples can navigate the wedding planning process with confidence, knowing that their privacy rights are respected and upheld at every stage.

Overreliance on Technology:

Myth: There's a misconception that the integration of AI may foster overreliance on technology, potentially diminishing couples' autonomy and decision-making capabilities.

Reality: AI acts as a tool to enhance rather than replace couples' decision-making processes. While AI facilitates data-driven insights and recommendations, the ultimate decision-making authority rests with the couple. By leveraging AI's analytical capabilities alongside their own intuition and preferences, couples can make informed choices that align with their vision for the wedding.

This collaborative approach ensures that technology enhances, rather than dictates, the planning process, empowering couples to create a celebration that authentically reflects their shared values and aspirations.

Cost Prohibitive:

Myth: There's a perception that AI-driven wedding planning solutions are financially out of reach for couples with modest budgets.

Reality: While AI technologies may entail initial investments, they often yield substantial returns in terms of cost savings and efficiency gains. Many AI platforms offer flexible pricing structures tailored to accommodate diverse budgetary constraints, making advanced planning tools accessible to couples across a wide spectrum of financial circumstances.

By embracing AI-powered solutions, couples can optimize resource allocation, mitigate unnecessary expenses, and maximize the value derived from every aspect of their wedding, thereby achieving a memorable celebration without compromising on quality or affordability.

Learning Curve and Accessibility:

Myth: Some may believe that AI-driven wedding planning tools require advanced technical skills and are inaccessible to those without a background in technology.

Reality: While AI technology may seem complex, many user-friendly platforms offer intuitive interfaces and comprehensive support resources to guide couples through the planning process. From tutorials and online guides to dedicated customer support channels, these resources ensure that users of all technical professions can leverage AI effectively.

Additionally, as AI becomes increasingly integrated into mainstream applications, its accessibility continues to improve, making advanced planning tools more approachable and user-friendly for a broader audience.

By addressing these common misconceptions, brides and wedding planners can approach AI with an open mind, ready to harness its full potential.

Now, let's turn our attention to the ethical considerations that come with using AI tools in wedding planning, ensuring that privacy and data security are maintained throughout the process.

Ethics: Privacy and Data Security in AI Tools

As we explore the benefits and dispel misconceptions, it's crucial to address the ethical considerations surrounding privacy and data security when utilizing AI tools in wedding planning. Ensuring ethical practices will help maintain trust and integrity throughout the planning process.

Data Privacy: Wedding planning involves sharing sensitive personal information, including preferences, contact details, and financial data. It is imperative that AI platforms handling this data adhere to stringent privacy protocols. Couples should ensure that their data is collected and stored securely, with clear policies in place regarding its usage and sharing. Transparent communication between couples and AI providers is essential to establish trust and ensure that privacy rights are respected throughout the planning process.

Informed Consent: It is important that couples have full transparency regarding how their data will be utilized by AI tools. This includes understanding the types of data collected, the purposes for which it will be used, and any third parties with whom it may be shared. Informed consent ensures that couples have control over their personal information and can make educated decisions about its use in their wedding planning journey.

Data Security: AI platforms must implement robust security measures to safeguard against data breaches and unauthorized access. This includes encryption of sensitive data, regular security audits, and adherence to industry best practices for cybersecurity. Couples should inquire about the security protocols employed by

AI providers and verify that their data is protected against potential threats.

Minimization of Data Collection: To mitigate privacy risks, AI tools should adopt the principle of data minimization, collecting only the information necessary for the planning process. Excessive data collection increases the likelihood of privacy breaches and may infringe upon couples rights to privacy. By limiting the scope of data collection to essential elements, AI platforms can uphold privacy standards while still delivering valuable insights and recommendations.

Anonymization and Aggregation: AI platforms can enhance privacy protections by anonymizing and aggregating data wherever possible. By removing personally identifiable information from datasets and analyzing data in aggregate, AI tools can generate valuable insights without compromising individual privacy. This approach ensures that couples' data remains confidential while still contributing to the overall efficacy of AI-driven planning solutions.

Ethical Use of AI Algorithms: AI algorithms should be designed and deployed ethically with a focus on fairness, transparency, and accountability. Biases within algorithms can lead to discriminatory outcomes, perpetuating inequalities and injustices. AI developers must prioritize fairness and inclusivity, regularly auditing algorithms for bias and implementing corrective measures where necessary. Additionally, transparency in algorithmic decision-making ensures that couples understand how recommendations are generated and can trust the integrity of the AI-driven planning process.

By prioritizing privacy and data security considerations, couples can leverage AI tools in wedding planning with confidence, knowing that their personal information is protected and their ethical values are upheld throughout the process. Open communication, informed consent, and robust security measures are essential pillars of ethical AI implementation in the context of wedding planning.

In summary, the integration of artificial intelligence (AI) into wedding planning represents a significant paradigm shift, ushering in a new era of efficiency, personalization, and innovation. By harnessing the capabilities of AI technologies, couples and planners can streamline operations, enhance creativity, and optimize resources to curate unforgettable celebrations of love. From automated task management to personalized recommendations and predictive planning, AI offers a myriad of benefits that empower couples to realize their dream weddings with greater ease and precision.

However, it's essential to address ethical considerations surrounding privacy, data security, and algorithmic bias in the use of AI tools. By prioritizing transparency, informed consent, and robust security measures, couples can ensure that their personal information is safeguarded throughout the planning process. Moreover, vigilance against algorithmic biases is crucial to promoting fairness and inclusivity in decision-making.

Despite these challenges, the potential of AI to transform wedding planning is undeniable. By dispelling common misconceptions and embracing AI as a valuable ally, couples can unlock a wealth of opportunities for creativity, efficiency, and personalization. Ultimately, AI enables couples to embark on a journey of crafting truly unique and memorable celebrations that reflect their love story in every detail. As AI continues to evolve, its role in wedding planning will undoubtedly evolve as well, offering even greater possibilities for couples to create the wedding of their dreams.

With a clear understanding of AI and its role in wedding planning, we can now move on to setting up your digital planning toolbox.

Alicia Hernandez-Whyle

Chapter Two

Setting Up Your Digital Planning Toolbox

In today's fast-paced, tech-savvy world, planning your wedding can be made exponentially easier with the right digital tools and strategies. Gone are the days when brides-to-be had to rely solely on bulky binders, endless paper lists, and countless phone calls to coordinate their big day. Now, with a plethora of apps, platforms, and smart devices at your fingertips, organizing every detail of your wedding can be streamlined into a seamless, efficient process.

This chapter is your ultimate guide to setting up a digital planning toolbox that will transform your wedding planning experience. We'll explore essential apps and tools specifically designed to meet the needs of brides-to-be, ensuring you have everything you need, from guest lists to vendor management. You'll learn how to integrate AI assistants and smart devices, allowing you to connect and optimize your smartphone, tablet, and smart home gadgets to stay on top of tasks effortlessly.

Additionally, we will provide a step-by-step guide to creating a digital workflow, ensuring smooth and efficient communication and task management with your wedding party, vendors, and loved ones. Also, because we know budgeting is crucial, we'll cover the cost considerations for the tools and subscriptions you might need, helping you make informed decisions without breaking the bank.

By the end of this chapter, you will be equipped with a comprehensive digital toolbox, ready to tackle every aspect of your wedding planning with confidence and ease. Let's dive in and start building the perfect digital foundation for your special day.

To get started, we will first explore a comprehensive list of recommended software and platforms that can aid in various aspects of your wedding planning.

Recommended AI software and platforms

While there isn't a single app that encompasses every feature mentioned below, several comprehensive wedding planning platforms offer a wide range of tools and services, making them versatile and efficient for most planning needs.

Here are some of the best all-in-one wedding planning apps:

The Knot offers a comprehensive wedding planning checklist, covering everything from selecting a venue to sending thank-you notes. Set reminders for important tasks like booking your venue and finalizing your guest list, ensuring no detail is overlooked. The service is free to use.

WeddingWire provides vendor reviews, wedding website templates, and budget planning tools. Read reviews from other couples to find reputable vendors, helping you make informed decisions and choose the best options for your wedding. This service is free of charge.

Zola streamlines the wedding planning process by combining registry services with planning tools like guest list management and checklist creation. Consolidate tasks on one platform to easily keep track of your progress and stay organized. Zola offers basic services for free, with premium options available starting at $19.99 per month.

Joy offers digital invitations, RSVP tracking, and a centralized hub for sharing wedding details with guests. Create a personalized wedding website where guests can find all the information they need, making it easier for them to plan and RSVP. This service is free to use.

Appy Couple provides stylish wedding website templates and guest communication tools. Share photos and updates with your guests, build excitement, and keep everyone informed about any changes or updates to your plans. Appy Couple's services start at $49, with premium packages available up to $149.

Budget Trackers

Mint offers a comprehensive view of your finances, allowing you to track spending and set budgets for different categories, including wedding expenses. Create a specific wedding budget and monitor your spending to stay within your means. Mint is available for free.

You Need a Budget (YNAB) encourages proactive budgeting by assigning dollars to specific categories and prioritizing spending. Allocate funds to your wedding budget and adjust as needed to cover all expenses without overspending. YNAB costs $14.99 per month or $98.99 per year.

Honeyfund provides a unique way to fund wedding expenses by allowing guests to contribute to your honeymoon or wedding fund as gifts. Create a honeymoon fund and share it with your guests for contributions to memorable experiences. Basic services on Honeyfund are free, with premium options available starting at $39.

Once your budget is in place, managing your guest list becomes the next crucial step. Here are some tools to help you streamline your guest list management.

Guest List Managers

AllSeated offers virtual seating chart creation and venue visualization tools, making it easy to plan your wedding layout. Create seating charts for your ceremony and reception, experiment with seating arrangements, and ensure every guest has a designated seat. AllSeated's services are free to use.

RSVPify streamlines the RSVP process by allowing guests to RSVP online and providing real-time updates on guest attendance. Create customizable RSVP forms, collect essential information, and track RSVPs, making it easier to plan and coordinate your wedding. RSVPify offers basic services for free, with premium options available starting at $29 per event.

Timeline Organizers

Trello uses visual boards and customizable workflows to organize and prioritize wedding tasks and deadlines. Create boards for different aspects of wedding planning, such as venue selection and vendor coordination, and use cards to track tasks and deadlines. Trello offers basic services for free, with premium options available starting at $12.50 per user per month.

Asana helps stay organized with task delegation and deadline management features. Create projects for different planning stages, assign tasks to the wedding party and vendors, set deadlines, and track progress to ensure timely completion of tasks. Asana provides basic services for free, with premium options available starting at $10.99 per user per month.

Aisle Planner provides a detailed timeline for your wedding day, ensuring everything runs smoothly. Create a timeline outlining key events and milestones, such as ceremony start time and reception entrance, and share it with your wedding party and vendors. Aisle Planner costs $39 per month.

WeddingWire Timeline Tool offers a customizable timeline to help stay on track with wedding planning. Set reminders for important tasks like booking the venue, sending invitations, and finalizing the wedding day timeline to ensure nothing is missed. This tool is free to use.

Google Calendar makes coordinating schedules and appointments easy with shared calendars and event scheduling. Create a shared calendar for wedding planning, add events for vendor meetings and dress fittings, and invite the wedding party and vendors to view and edit. Google Calendar is free to use.

In addition to managing timelines, generating fresh and creative ideas for your wedding is essential. The following AI tools can help you brainstorm and design your perfect wedding.

Wedding Idea Generation: AI Tools

ChatGPT assists with brainstorming ideas, answering questions, and providing creative solutions. Use ChatGPT to generate themes, suggest unique decoration ideas, and help draft wedding vows or speeches. This service offers basic features for free, with premium options available starting at $20 per month.

Claude excels in providing personalized suggestions and creative input. It is useful for planning events by offering tailored recommendations based on preferences and style, helping brainstorm innovative concepts for the ceremony and reception. Claude offers basic services for free, with premium options available starting at $25 per month.

Canva's Design offers inspiration and suggestions for wedding invitations, save-the-dates, and other graphics with AI-powered design tools. Use Canva's templates and design elements to visualize and create beautiful wedding materials. Canva provides basic services for free, with premium options available starting at $12.95 per month.

Pinterest Lens uses image recognition to discover inspiration from photos. Snap a picture of something you like, and Pinterest Lens will show similar images and ideas, aiding in gathering decor and style inspiration. This tool is free to use.

AI Assistants and Smart Devices in Wedding Planning

Voice Commands with AI Assistants: Use voice-activated assistants like Alexa, Google Assistant, Siri, and Cortana to perform tasks hands-free. Examples include adding tasks to your to-do list, setting reminders for deadlines, and researching wedding ideas and vendors using voice search.

Smartphone and Tablet Apps: Utilize wedding planning apps on your devices for features like checklists, budget trackers, guest list managers, and virtual wedding dress try-ons. These apps provide comprehensive assistance throughout the planning process.

Syncing Across Devices: Ensure all your devices are synced and connected to the same accounts and platforms for seamless access to planning tools and information, whether at home, on the go, or at vendor meetings.

Smart Home Integration: Integrate smart home gadgets such as speakers, lights, and cameras to enhance your planning environment. Use smart lighting to set the mood while brainstorming and smart cameras to document your planning journey with high-quality photos and videos.

Automation and Reminders: Leverage automation to simplify repetitive tasks and set reminders for important milestones. Automate smart home devices to adjust settings based on your routine and set reminders for vendor appointments and payments.

Chatbots and Virtual Assistants: Use AI-powered chatbots and virtual assistants like ChatGPT or Claude for instant support and to answer wedding planning questions. Integrate these tools into your wedding website or social media platforms for round-the-clock assistance.

Natural Language Processing (NLP) Tools: Tools like Grammarly or Hemingway can help craft eloquent and error-free wedding invitations, speeches, and other written materials by analyzing text for grammar, style, and readability.

Image Recognition Technology: Utilize image recognition tools such as Google Lens or Pinterest Lens to identify and gather inspiration from wedding-related photos. Snap a photo of a floral arrangement or decor idea, and these tools will search the web for similar images and related content.

Data Analytics Platforms: Platforms like Google Analytics or social media insights tools provide valuable insights into your wedding planning efforts by tracking website traffic, social media engagement, and email campaign performance, helping you tailor your strategy.

Virtual Reality (VR) and Augmented Reality (AR): Use VR and AR technologies to visualize and plan wedding aspects. Tour potential venues remotely with VR, or use AR to preview decor elements in your chosen space.

Sentiment Analysis Tools: Tools like **Brandwatch** or **Hootsuite** Insights monitor social media conversations and online reviews. Analyzing sentiment helps gauge overall feelings towards your wedding plans, allowing adjustments to ensure a positive experience for everyone involved.

By effectively integrating these AI assistants and smart devices, you can optimize efficiency, stay organized, and reduce stress, focusing on creating the wedding of your dreams.

Now that we've covered the essential digital tools and resources, let's move on to how you can create a digital workflow. This step-by-step guide will help you establish a smooth and efficient planning process.

Step-by-Step Guide to Creating a Digital Workflow

Planning a wedding involves meticulous coordination and clear communication. Establishing a digital workflow with shared calendars, task management apps, and communication protocols can streamline the process. This approach enhances organization, productivity, and efficiency, helping you plan your dream wedding effortlessly.

Step 1: Assess Your Needs

Before selecting digital tools, it's crucial to understand your specific wedding planning requirements. Consider factors such as the size and complexity of your wedding, the number of vendors involved, and the preferences of your wedding party.

Identify Key Tasks: Start by listing all the tasks involved in planning your wedding. Consider everything, from booking the venue to selecting the music playlist.

Determine Communication Channels: Assess the various communication channels you'll need to utilize, such as email, messaging apps, video conferencing, and social media. For instance, you may prefer email for formal communications with vendors and messaging apps like WhatsApp or Slack for quick updates on your wedding party.

Step 2: Choose Collaboration Tools

Selecting the right AI tools is essential for effective communication and teamwork. Consider factors such as ease of use, compatibility with existing systems, and features tailored to wedding planning needs. Let's explore the various communication tools that can enhance collaboration and efficiency in wedding planning.

Slack: Create dedicated channels for different aspects of wedding planning, such as venue, catering, and entertainment. Utilize features like file sharing and integrations with other tools to streamline communication.

Microsoft Teams: Leverage Teams' chat, video conferencing, and document collaboration capabilities to facilitate seamless communication among your wedding party and vendors.

ChatGPT: Use ChatGPT to brainstorm ideas, get personalized recommendations, and clarify any doubts throughout the planning process.

Trello: Trello is an excellent tool for visual task management. Create boards for each aspect of your wedding (e.g., venue, guest list, vendors) and assign tasks with due dates.

Zoom: This AI-powered virtual assistant can schedule meetings, send reminders, and even conduct basic research, saving you time and effort.

Google Assistant: Integrate Google Assistant with your calendar to set reminders, manage appointments, and send quick messages.

Canva: Canva's AI-powered design tools can help you create beautiful invitations, save-the-dates, and other graphics for your wedding.

Step 3: Implement Shared Calendars

Shared calendars help keep everyone informed about important dates, appointments, and deadlines. Choose a platform that allows for easy sharing and syncing across devices. Here are some platform tools to consider:

Google Calendar: Create separate calendars for different aspects of your wedding, such as vendor meetings, dress fittings, and rehearsal dinners. Share these calendars with your wedding party and vendors, allowing everyone to stay updated on scheduling conflicts and availability.

Microsoft Outlook: Share your calendar with specific individuals or groups, granting them access to view and edit events. Utilize features like color-coding and reminders to stay organized and on schedule. You can create categories for different types of events, such as meetings, appointments, and deadlines, and color-code them accordingly for easy identification.

Step 4: Utilize Task Management Apps

Task management apps streamline task delegation, tracking, and collaboration. Look for apps that offer features such as to-do lists, reminders, and progress tracking. Consider the following task management app to aid with wedding planning.

Asana: Create projects for different aspects of wedding planning, such as venue selection, decor, and entertainment. Break down tasks into actionable steps, assign due dates, and monitor progress using visual project boards. For instance, create a project titled "Floral Arrangements" and assign tasks such as researching florists, obtaining quotes, and finalizing arrangements.

Todoist: Compile a comprehensive to-do list for your wedding, categorizing tasks by priority and due date. Set recurring tasks for routine activities, such as vendor follow-ups or budget reviews, and utilize features like labels and filters to organize tasks effectively. For example, create a recurring task titled "Check Budget" to review your wedding expenses every week and adjust your spending as needed.

Step 5: Establish Communication Protocols

Clear communication protocols are essential for ensuring effective collaboration and minimizing misunderstandings. Establish guidelines for preferred communication channels, response times, and escalation procedures.

Define Preferred Communication Channels: Determine which communication channels will be used for different types of communication, such as email for formal communications with vendors and messaging apps for quick updates.

Set Response Time Expectations: Establish expectations for response times to messages and emails, ensuring timely communication and reducing delays in decision-making. For instance, agree upon a maximum response time of 24 hours for non-urgent messages and emails, and designate specific times for checking and responding to communication during the day.

Outline Escalation Procedures: Define procedures for escalating urgent issues or concerns, specifying who should be contacted and how they can be reached in case of emergencies. For example, create a contact list with phone numbers and email addresses of key stakeholders, such as your wedding planner, venue coordinator, and emergency contacts, and share it with your wedding party and vendors for easy reference.

Step 6: Provide Training and Support

Offering training and support ensures that everyone involved in the wedding planning process feels comfortable using digital tools effectively.

Training Sessions: Conduct training sessions or workshops to familiarize your wedding party and vendors with the chosen digital tools. For example, organize a virtual training session via Zoom to walk your bridesmaids through using the shared calendar and task management app, answering any questions they may have along the way.

Provide Resources: Offer resources such as user guides and tutorials to support ongoing learning and troubleshooting. Encourage individuals to explore the tools on their own and seek assistance when needed. You can create a dedicated webpage or Google Drive folder with instructional materials and useful resources for easy access by your wedding party and vendors.

Offer Ongoing Support: Be available to answer questions and provide support as needed throughout the planning process. Foster an environment where individuals feel comfortable reaching out for help and sharing feedback on their experiences with the digital workflow. Schedule regular check-ins or office hours where individuals can ask questions, share updates, and receive guidance on using the digital tools effectively.

Step 7: Regularly Review and Adapt

Regularly reviewing and adapting your digital workflow ensures that it remains effective and aligned with your evolving needs and preferences.

Feedback Sessions: Schedule regular feedback sessions with your wedding party and vendors to gather insights and identify areas for improvement. Encourage open and honest communication about what's working well and what could be enhanced. For example, organize a monthly virtual meeting with your wedding party to discuss any challenges or issues encountered with the digital workflow and brainstorm potential solutions.

Monitor Performance Metrics: Track key performance metrics such as response times, task completion rates, and overall satisfaction with the digital workflow. Use this data to identify trends and make informed decisions about adjustments and optimizations. You can create surveys or use built-in analytics tools in your collaboration platforms to collect feedback and measure performance.

Iterate and Improve: Continuously iterate and improve your digital workflow based on the feedback received and performance insights gathered. Be open to experimenting with new tools and approaches to find the optimal solution for your wedding planning needs. For example, if you notice that certain communication channels are underutilized or causing confusion, consider switching to alternative platforms or adjusting your communication protocols accordingly.

By following this comprehensive guide and incorporating detailed examples, you can create a robust digital workflow that enhances communication, collaboration, and productivity throughout your wedding planning journey.

Security and Privacy Best Practices

When using digital tools, it's essential to ensure the security and privacy of your data.

Data Encryption: Ensure that the tools you use offer data encryption to protect your personal and financial information.

Strong Passwords: Use strong, unique passwords for each tool and platform. Consider using a password manager to keep track of them.

Two-Factor Authentication: Enable two-factor authentication (2FA) for an added layer of security.

Regular Backups: Regularly back up your data to prevent loss due to technical issues or cyberattacks.

Privacy Settings: Review and adjust the privacy settings on your digital tools to control who can access your information.

Finally, it's crucial to consider the costs associated with these digital tools and subscriptions. Here's how to budget effectively for your tech needs.

Budgeting for Tech: Tools and Subscription Costs

When budgeting for technology tools and subscriptions, it's essential to ensure you get the best value and functionality. Here are some tips to help you make informed decisions:

Evaluate Features: Look closely at what each tool offers. Beyond the basics, consider advanced features, customization options, and additional modules. Compare different tools to find the best fit for your needs.

Consider Scalability: Ensure the tools can grow with your needs. If you're working with a team, assess how many user licenses you'll need. Some tools charge per user, while others have fixed costs. Choose the most cost-efficient option.

Subscription Models and Billing Cycles: Decide whether monthly or annual subscriptions work best. Annual plans often come with discounts. Be aware of fees for early cancellation, especially if you're unsure about long-term use.

Integration and Compatibility: Ensure the tools can integrate with your existing systems. Check for extra costs or technical challenges in integrating different tools. Built-in integrations are usually simpler and more cost-effective.

Training and Support: Good training and support are crucial. Look for tools with high-quality training resources like user guides, tutorials, and customer support. Check if there are extra costs for training sessions or premium support.

Return on Investment: Estimate the return on investment by comparing the tool's costs to the time and money it saves compared to manual methods.

By keeping these tips in mind, you can choose the best tech tools and subscriptions for your wedding planning, ensuring you get the most value and efficiency.

To conclude, in the modern, fast-paced world, planning a wedding becomes much easier with the right digital tools and strategies. By setting up a comprehensive digital planning toolbox, you can streamline every aspect of your wedding planning. From managing guest lists and vendor communications to creating timelines and tracking your budget, these tools make the process more efficient and stress-free.

Alicia Hernandez-Whyle

This chapter has equipped you with a wealth of knowledge on essential apps and platforms specifically designed for brides-to-be. You've learned how to integrate AI assistants and smart devices, allowing you to connect and optimize your smartphone, tablet, and smart home gadgets to stay on top of tasks effortlessly. We have also provided a step-by-step guide to creating a digital workflow, ensuring smooth and efficient communication and task management with your wedding party, vendors, and loved ones.

By following the insights and recommendations provided, you can enhance organization, productivity, and efficiency, ultimately reducing stress and allowing you to focus on the joy of planning your special day. From choosing the right tools and budgeting for subscriptions to establishing communication protocols and providing ongoing support, this chapter has laid the foundation for a seamless, tech-enhanced wedding planning experience.

As you continue your wedding planning journey, remember that the goal is to create a celebration that reflects your unique vision and love story. With your digital planning toolbox in place, you are well-equipped to tackle every challenge with confidence and ease. Embrace the power of technology to make your wedding planning as magical and memorable as the day itself.

Part Two: Planning with Precision

Alicia Hernandez-Whyle

Chapter Three

Budgeting: Keeping Costs Under Control

When it comes to wedding planning, setting a budget is the first and most critical step. A well-thought-out budget provides a financial framework and helps prioritize what matters most to you and your partner. This chapter, "Budgeting: Keeping Costs Under Control," will guide you through defining your wedding vision, establishing a budget, and how AI can streamline the process.

In today's digital age, AI applications are revolutionizing traditional wedding budgeting. Imagine having a personal financial advisor at your fingertips who understands your needs, predicts potential expenses, and helps you make informed decisions. AI offers innovative solutions that ensure your wedding plans remain on track and within budget.

From intelligent budget tracking to personalized expense forecasting, the integration of AI technology is redefining how couples manage their wedding budgets. Whether you're dreaming of a grand celebration or an intimate gathering, the right tools can make the difference between financial stress and a smooth, enjoyable planning experience.

Prepare to discover a range of AI-powered tools and strategies that will empower you to take charge of your wedding budget with confidence. By the end of this chapter, you'll understand your financial landscape and know how to leverage technology for a seamless, stress-free wedding planning journey.

Defining Your Wedding Vision

Before diving into numbers, it's crucial to define your wedding vision. This involves envisioning the style, size, and overall ambiance of your wedding. Here's how to start:

Venue Type: Do you prefer an indoor or outdoor venue? A ballroom or a beach? Think about the atmosphere you want to create and how it aligns with your wedding vision. Additionally, consider the season and weather, as these factors can greatly impact your venue choice.

Guest List: How many guests are you planning to invite? Your guest list will shape many aspects of your wedding, from the venue size to the catering requirements. Take time to create a list that includes everyone you want to share your special day with, and be prepared to make adjustments as needed.

Theme and Style: Are you aiming for a traditional, modern, rustic, or themed wedding? Your wedding style will significantly impact your budget, as different styles come with varying costs for decor, attire, and venues.

Key Priorities: What aspects of the wedding are most important to you? Identify your top priorities, whether it's the venue, food, photography, or entertainment. Knowing what matters most will help you allocate your budget more effectively and ensure that your wedding reflects your vision and values.

Having a clear vision helps you prioritize your spending and allocate your budget effectively. Once you have a clear vision, the next step is to establish a realistic budget.

Establishing a Budget

Begin by thoroughly assessing your financial situation. Look into your savings, including any joint accounts with your partner, and evaluate your monthly income against expenses. Be realistic about what you can save each month without compromising your financial stability. Additionally, take stock of any existing debt and aim to plan a wedding budget that avoids accumulating further debt.

Once you have a clear understanding of your financial standing, consider potential sources of funding. Personal savings are often the primary source, so review your accounts to see how much you can allocate to your wedding expenses. Discuss with family members about potential contributions, as parents or relatives may be willing to assist financially. Keep in mind gifts received from engagement parties or pre-wedding events, as these could also contribute to your budget. Explore alternative funding methods cautiously, such as personal loans or crowdfunding platforms.

Once you have set a total budget for your wedding, the next step is to allocate funds across various categories.

Allocating Funds: Essential Budget Categories

Properly dividing your budget helps ensure that all aspects of your wedding are covered and that you can prioritize what's most important to you. A comprehensive list of categories to consider is provided for you at the back of this book. After identifying all potential expenses, prioritize the categories that are most important to you. For example, if photography is a top priority, allocate a larger portion of your budget to it. Here is a general guideline for allocation percentages. Adjust them based on your priorities:

Venue and Catering: 40-50%

Attire and Accessories: 10-15%

Photography and Videography: 10-12%

Entertainment: 8-10%

Flowers and Décor: 8-10%

Stationery: 2-4%

Transportation: 2-3%

Rings: 2-3%

Gifts and Favors: 1-2%

Miscellaneous: 5-10%

Ensuring flexibility in your budget allows you to handle unexpected costs and adjustments smoothly.

With your budget established and allocated, it's important to plan for the unexpected by creating a contingency fund.

Creating a Contingency Fund

Planning your dream wedding involves managing a budget to cover essential expenses like the venue, dress, and decorations. However, unforeseen costs can pop up, causing stress and financial strain. A contingency fund serves as a safety net for these unexpected expenses without derailing your plans. Set aside around 15-20% of your total budget for the contingency fund for unforeseen expenses. This extra cushion provides peace of mind throughout the planning process.

Set up automatic transfers on a monthly basis to your contingency fund. This ensures consistent savings without active effort.

Ensure your budget and contingency fund remain sufficient. Communicate openly with vendors and your wedding planner about budget constraints. They may offer helpful suggestions to help you stay within your budget and avoid unexpected expenses.

To ensure financial stability throughout your planning, it's essential to master wedding finances by tracking hidden costs and payments.

Alicia Hernandez-Whyle

Managing Wedding Expenses

Be aware of hidden costs like service charges, taxes, gratuities, overtime fees, and vendor transportation. These can add up and impact your budget. Try to anticipate where unexpected costs might arise during wedding planning to better prepare and allocate funds.

Tracking payments and due dates is crucial to ensuring everything stays on track and within budget. Start by setting up a comprehensive spreadsheet or using a wedding planning app like **WeddingWire** to track all payments and due dates. Include columns for the vendor name, service or item, payment amount, due date, and payment status. This centralized system allows you to easily monitor your financial obligations and stay organized throughout the planning process.

Set reminders, alerts, or notifications for at least a week before each payment is due to give yourself enough time to gather funds and submit payments. This proactive approach helps prevent missed deadlines and late fees.

Make it a habit to regularly review your payment tracker to ensure all payments are up-to-date and accounted for. This ongoing monitoring allows you to identify any discrepancies or outstanding balances early on, giving you time to address them before they become problematic.

By implementing these strategies for tracking payments and due dates, you can effectively manage your wedding finances and ensure that all vendors are paid on time.

With a solid grasp on tracking costs and payments, let's explore how using AI for budget setting can streamline your wedding planning process.

Using AI for Budget Setting

AI-powered tools can be game-changers in setting and managing your wedding budget. Let us look at how these tools offer a range of features that help streamline the budgeting process, making it more accurate and less stressful.

Realistic Budget Estimation: AI tools can analyze your financial data, such as income, savings, and spending habits, to suggest a budget that fits your financial capacity. They consider your wedding vision and preferences and allocate funds accordingly, ensuring that you don't overspend while still achieving your dream wedding.

Personalized Budget Plans: Based on your inputs and preferences, AI can create a tailored budget plan that prioritizes the elements most important to you, such as the venue, catering, or entertainment. This helps you allocate your resources effectively, ensuring a balanced approach to spending.

Comparative Analysis: AI tools can access a vast database of previous weddings to compare costs and trends. This allows you to benchmark your budget against similar weddings, giving you a realistic perspective on what to expect and how to allocate funds efficiently.

These tools offer a range of features, from budgeting and expense tracking to personalized recommendations and real-time monitoring. Here are some AI tools that can help with wedding budget planning and allocation:

AI Tools for Wedding Budget Management

WeddingWire Budget Planner: This tool offers a tailored budgeting tool for weddings, breaking down expenses into categories like venue, catering, and attire. It suggests realistic budgets based on historical data and tracks expenses in real-time, alerting users if they near budget limits. Ideal for couples, the WeddingWire Budget Planner provides detailed tracking, AI-driven advice, and streamlines budget management for financial transparency.

Mint: This popular personal finance tool can be customized for wedding budgeting. It offers holistic management of income, expenses, and overall financial health. With AI features analyzing spending habits, Mint provides recommendations on fund allocation and categorizes expenses, alerting users to potential overspending. Ideal for couples, Mint ensures financial organization and control for both wedding and personal finances.

Zola Budget Tool: It is designed for weddings, providing detailed cost estimates based on wedding size and style. Its AI features offer tailored budgeting recommendations, dynamically adjusting as real costs are inputted and tracking spending in real-time. Perfect for couples seeking a dedicated wedding planning platform, Zola ensures seamless budget management and financial transparency.

You Need A Budget (YNAB): This is a personal finance tool that can be adapted for wedding budgeting by creating specific categories. Its AI features offer real-time tracking and overspending alerts, ensuring financial discipline. AI-driven insights help allocate funds efficiently, making it ideal for couples preferring a detailed, rule-based budgeting system.

The Knot Budget Calculator: A wedding-specific budget calculator that manages and tracks expenses across categories. Its AI features suggest budgets based on wedding size, location, and style, ensuring accurate planning and financial transparency. Perfect for couples wanting a straightforward, wedding-focused budget tool.

PlanIt: This is a comprehensive wedding planning app with budgeting tools, timelines, and vendor management. Its AI capabilities suggest optimal spending categories and track progress in real-time. Ideal for couples seeking a full-featured planning app with robust budget management.

Personal Capital: This finance management tool is available on the app store and can be adapted for wedding budgeting, offering a detailed financial overview. Its AI features analyze spending patterns and suggest saving opportunities, aligning wedding budgeting with broader financial goals. Suitable for couples integrating wedding and overall financial planning.

Honeyfund: Honeyfund, primarily known for its honeymoon registry, also offers a robust wedding planning and budget management tool. Its AI features help manage contributions and expenses, provide insights into budget allocation, and suggest cost-saving opportunities. Ideal for couples wanting to manage both wedding and honeymoon expenses in one place, Honeyfund ensures streamlined budget management and financial organization for a stress-free planning experience.

ChatGPT/Bard: These provide personalized wedding budget recommendations, cost-saving strategies, and idea generation, ideal for tailored budgeting and planning advice. Bard (Google AI) excels in generating creative ideas and budget insights, offering affordable planning tips and deal-finding assistance through Google's platform, ensuring innovative budgeting solutions.

Jasper/Perplexity: Jasper AI provides comprehensive wedding planning and budgeting assistance, generating budgets, budget-friendly ideas, and vendor communication drafts via subscription. Perplexity AI offers quick answers, pricing information, and concise cost comparisons without a subscription. Both tools provide innovative, budget-friendly ideas, creative suggestions, and cost-saving tips across various wedding categories.

To illustrate the practical benefits of AI tools, let's delve into Alisha and Bryan's Honeyfund experience.

Alisha and Bryan's Honeyfund Experience

Background:

Alicia Hernandez-Whyle

Alisha and Bryan, a young couple deeply in love, dreamed of having a beautiful wedding celebration but were concerned about the financial strain it might bring. They were determined to plan their wedding smartly without compromising on their vision. They decided to explore innovative ways to manage their wedding budget and stumbled upon Honeyfund, primarily known for its honeymoon registry but also offering a comprehensive wedding planning and budget management tool.

Solution:

Alisha and Bryan were drawn to Honeyfund's reputation for simplifying the financial aspects of wedding planning, so they decided to give it a try. With Honeyfund, they found a seamless platform that not only allowed them to create a honeymoon registry but also provided robust budget management features. They were able to set up their wedding budget easily within the platform, allocating funds to different categories such as venue, catering, attire, and decorations.

Outcome:

Using Honeyfund, Alisha and Bryan experienced a stress-free wedding planning journey. The platform's AI-driven features helped them manage contributions and expenses effectively, providing insights into budget allocation and suggesting cost-saving opportunities along the way. They were able to track their spending in real-time, ensuring they stayed within their budget without sacrificing their wedding vision.

Furthermore, Honeyfund's integration of honeymoon registry and wedding planning tools proved to be a game-changer for Alisha and Bryan. They were able to manage both their wedding and honeymoon expenses in one place, streamlining their financial organization and simplifying the planning process.

On their wedding day, Alisha and Bryan were able to celebrate with joy and peace of mind, knowing that they had managed their budget wisely with the help of Honeyfund. The platform not only provided financial assistance but also contributed to their overall wedding experience by offering innovative solutions tailored to their needs.

For Alisha and Bryan, Honeyfund was more than just a wedding planning tool; it was a trusted companion that helped them navigate the complexities of wedding budget management with ease. Through personalized recommendations, seamless integration of wedding and honeymoon planning features, and real-time financial tracking, Honeyfund ensured that Alisha and Bryan could focus on what truly mattered: celebrating their love surrounded by family and friends, without the burden of financial stress.

Building on Alisha and Bryan's experience, let's explore the steps for choosing the right AI tool to aid with your wedding budget.

Steps for Choosing the Right AI tool for Your Wedding Budget

Step 1: Define Your Needs: Determine what aspects of your wedding budget you need the most help with, such as setting a budget, finding cost-saving opportunities, or tracking expenses.

Step 2: Choose the Right Tool: Select an AI tool that best fits your needs. For example, use ChatGPT for general advice and Jasper AI for detailed budget breakdowns.

Step 3: Set Up Your Budget: Use tools like The Knot or YNAB AI to create and manage your budget, ensuring all categories are covered.

Step 4: Seek Continuous Advice: Regularly consult AI tools like ChatGPT for ongoing recommendations and to answer any new questions that arise during the planning process.

Step 5: Monitor and Adjust: Use real-time tracking tools to monitor your spending and adjust your budget as needed to stay within your financial limits.

In addition to AI tools, using interactive budget templates can further streamline your wedding planning process.

Using Interactive Budget Templates

Interactive budget templates are invaluable tools in wedding planning, offering a seamless way to manage finances. These templates are user-friendly, with pre-formatted fields for expenses, eliminating the need for manual entry. Couples can input their financial data, allowing the template to automatically organize and categorize expenses.

Customization options enable couples to tailor the template to their specific needs, adjusting categories or incorporating unique expenses. This flexibility ensures the budgeting process aligns with their wedding vision.

Numerous downloadable templates are available on sites like **ExcelTemplate.net, Etsy, Vertex42,** and **TemplateLab** in formats such as **Excel, Google Sheets**, and **PDF**. By leveraging these interactive templates, couples can simplify wedding budgeting and optimize financial resources.

In conclusion, the role of a well-managed budget cannot be overstated. Throughout this chapter, "Budgeting: Keeping Costs Under Control," we have seen how integrating artificial intelligence can transform the budgeting process from a potential source of stress into a smooth, manageable, and even enjoyable part of your wedding journey.

AI tools such as **ChatGPT, Jasper AI,** and **Bard** bring a level of personalized financial planning that was once only available through professional advisors. They help you set realistic budgets based on your unique vision and financial situation, provide insightful cost-saving tips, and allow for dynamic adjustments as your plans evolve.

Moreover, tools like **The Knot, YNAB,** and **Honeyfund** offer comprehensive solutions for budget tracking and management. These applications enable you to break down your budget into detailed categories, track real-time expenses, and provide alerts to keep you within your financial limits.

As we move towards a future where technology increasingly shapes our lives, leveraging AI for wedding budgeting empowers you to plan your special day with confidence and precision. These tools provide the support you need to navigate the financial complexities of wedding planning, allowing you to focus on creating a memorable and joyful celebration. By embracing AI, you not only ensure financial control but also enhance your overall planning experience, making it more organized, stress-free, and ultimately more enjoyable.

With the insights and tools provided in this chapter, you are well-equipped to take charge of your wedding budget while maintaining financial harmony.

Chapter Four

Venue Selection: Finding the Perfect Spot

Choosing the right venue for your wedding is one of the most crucial decisions in your planning journey. It's not just about finding a beautiful spot; it's about selecting a location that fits your vision, accommodates your guests, and aligns with your budget. The venue sets the tone for the entire event, influencing the atmosphere, style, and logistics of your special day.

Alicia Hernandez-Whyle

Whether you're dreaming of a rustic barn, a chic urban loft, or a serene beach setting, the venue determines the event's style, decor, and formality. A well-chosen venue can elevate your wedding from an ordinary event to an extraordinary experience that reflects your unique love story.

In the past, selecting a venue meant days of visiting different locations, comparing offerings, and negotiating contracts. Today, technology has streamlined this process, making it more accessible. This chapter will explore the modern approach to venue selection, emphasizing the importance of leveraging tools like virtual tours and AI-powered recommendations to simplify and enhance your decision-making.

With these considerations in mind, it's essential to utilize the latest advancements in technology to make the venue selection process more efficient and tailored to your specific needs. This brings us to the innovative world of AI-powered venue recommendations.

AI-Powered Venue Recommendations

Artificial intelligence is transforming the wedding planning landscape by providing sophisticated tools that analyze your preferences and budget to suggest the best venues. These AI tools take into account various factors such as location, style, and capacity, offering personalized recommendations that save you time and effort. They also provide insights into pricing and availability, helping you make informed decisions.

For example, **ChatGPT** (OpenAI) offers personalized venue suggestions based on your preferences and budget, providing detailed information about each venue, including pricing and availability. **Jasper** AI provides comprehensive venue recommendations, factoring in style, location, and capacity, and can even draft communication with venue vendors. **Bard** (Google AI) delivers creative and budget-friendly venue options, giving you a range of choices and highlighting deals or promotions that fit your criteria. These AI tools streamline the venue selection process, ensuring you find the perfect location for your special day.

With an understanding of how AI can simplify and enhance the venue selection process, let's delve into the specifics of how these AI tools operate to provide such tailored and efficient recommendations.

How AI Works in Venue Selection

AI technology can simplify finding the perfect wedding venue for you. Tools like **VenueFinder**, **EventUp** and **Modsy** start by gathering details about your wedding preferences, such as style, budget, location, guest count, and specific needs. They then match your profile with an extensive, updated database of venues using smart algorithms. The AI prioritizes what's most important to you, like budget or style, and refines its suggestions based on your feedback. These tools also use real-time data to ensure accurate, up-to-date information on venue availability and pricing, giving you reliable and relevant recommendations.

With AI simplifying the process, let's now explore how combining virtual tours with AI-powered recommendations offers an immersive and efficient approach to venue selection.

Modern Approach: Virtual Tours and AI Venue Recommendations

Traditionally, venue selection involved numerous site visits, extensive travel, and considerable time. However, modern technology has revolutionized this process, making it more convenient and efficient.

Virtual Tours

Virtual tours allow you to explore wedding venues from home with realistic 360-degree views, eliminating the need for physical visits. This is especially useful for destination weddings, saving time and money. You can visualize different setups, get a feel for the layout, and even take a virtual walk down the aisle. Couples can quickly view multiple venues, freeing up time for other planning tasks and reallocating travel savings to other parts of the wedding budget. Virtual tours offer flexibility, allowing you to visit venues anytime without coordinating with staff or taking time off work, which is great for busy couples or those planning distant weddings. You can explore venues at your own pace, make informed decisions, and compare options without the pressure of a sales pitch.

The technology behind virtual tours is sophisticated yet user-friendly, offering an immersive viewing experience. **360-degree cameras** capture spherical images, allowing viewers to explore the space from different angles.

How Virtual Tours for Wedding Venues Work

Access Online: Visit the website of the wedding venue offering virtual tours.

Launch Tour: Click on the virtual tour link or button to start.

Explore: Use your mouse or touchscreen to navigate through the venue. You can look around with 360-degree views.

Visualize Setups: Check different setups, like ceremony and reception areas, to see how they would look.

Feel the Layout: Get a sense of the venue's size and layout as you walk through it.

Compare and Decide: View multiple venues quickly, compare options, and make informed decisions without leaving home.

Virtual Reality (VR) enhances the experience by immersing viewers in the venue using headsets, with tools like Google VR Tours enabling couples to "visit" venues as if they were physically there, even from different countries. Combined with AI-powered tools, virtual tours offer a comprehensive and personalized approach to finding the perfect wedding venue, making it easier for couples to realize their wedding vision.

Having explored the advanced tools and methods for selecting the perfect wedding venue, let's now dive into a real-life story of destination wedding planning to see these strategies in action.

Real Life Story: Destination Wedding Planning

Sarah and John had always dreamed of a destination wedding in Italy, envisioning their special day amidst the romantic backdrop of historic villas and elegant palaces. However, their work commitments and ongoing travel restrictions made it impossible for them to visit potential venues in person.

Determined not to let these obstacles dampen their spirits, they turned to virtual tours. From the comfort of their home, Sarah and John embarked on a digital journey through Italy. They explored a variety of stunning venues, from charming historic villas nestled in the rolling hills of Tuscany to grand palaces in the heart of Rome. Each virtual tour provided them with detailed, realistic views, allowing them to get a true sense of the ambiance and layout of each location.

After thorough exploration and countless hours spent 'walking' through these beautiful venues, Sarah and John were able to narrow down their options to two favorites. They felt confident in their choices, having seen every detail up close without the need for a single site visit. The virtual tours not only saved them time and money but also brought their dream wedding one step closer to reality.

Sarah and John experience illustrates the transformative power of virtual tours in the wedding planning process, making it easier, faster, and more efficient for couples to find their perfect venue.

Now that we've discussed how to easily see venue virtually, let's delve into key considerations for selecting your venue.

Alicia Hernandez-Whyle

Key Features to Consider for the Perfect Venue

Once you have a shortlist of potential venues, the next step is to compare them to see which one best suits your needs.

Booking Timelines and Timing Considerations

Timing is everything when it comes to booking your venue. Popular venues book up quickly, often a year or more in advance, especially during peak wedding seasons. Understanding the optimal time to book and being flexible with your dates can increase your chances of securing your dream venue. Additionally, consider how the timing of your booking can affect your budget, with off-season dates often offering significant savings.

Style and Ambiance

The style and ambiance of your venue are crucial, as they set the tone for your wedding, reflecting your personal taste and creating the desired atmosphere. Choose a venue that complements your wedding theme, whether rustic charm, modern elegance, or classic sophistication. Consider the amount of decorating needed; some venues have inherent beauty and require minimal decor, while others might need more work to match your theme.

The ambiance should align with the emotional tone you want, whether it's a romantic garden, a chic urban loft, or a grand ballroom. Customization potential and flexibility in decor can significantly influence the overall feel of the wedding.

Seasonal Suitability and Personal Connection

When selecting a wedding venue, consider the season and weather conditions to ensure comfort and preparedness for any climate, especially for outdoor venues that require backup plans for inclement weather.

AI tools like **AccuWeather** use historical weather data and predictive modeling to advise on the best time of year for your chosen venue. They help you select a venue that is suitable for your wedding date, considering seasonal weather patterns and ensuring comfort for your guests.

Understanding the Importance of Capacity

The venue's capacity is also important as it determines if it can comfortably accommodate your guest list. A venue that is too small may lead to a cramped setting, while one that is too large can result in a lack of intimacy and higher costs. It is essential to estimate your guest count and ensure the venue's capacity aligns with this number.

Evaluating the Layout

The layout of the venue impacts the flow and functionality of the event. Key aspects to consider include accommodating various seating styles, such as round tables, banquet seating, or informal arrangements. Confirm that the dance floor and stage are appropriately sized and positioned for entertainment. Evaluate the ease of movement for guests, including those with disabilities, by checking for accessible restrooms, ramps, and elevators.

Additionally, consider if the venue offers separate spaces for different parts of your celebration, such as a cocktail area, dining space, and ceremony site, to ensure a smooth transition between events.

Services

Some venues offer in-house catering or have preferred vendors, simplifying planning but potentially limiting choices. Check if the venue provides decor items like tables, chairs, linens, and lighting, or if you need to arrange these separately. Venues may include Audiovisual equipment like microphones, projectors, and sound systems, essential for speeches and entertainment.

Additionally, some venues offer on-site coordinators to assist with logistics on the day of the event, ensuring everything runs smoothly.

Amenities

Ensure ample parking is available, including valet services or shuttle transportation if necessary. Check the number and condition of restrooms to accommodate your guest list. For out-of-town guests, consider on-site accommodations or nearby hotel partnerships.

Location and Transportation

The location of the wedding venue plays a crucial role in guest convenience and accessibility. Selecting a venue close to accommodations where guests can stay is advantageous, as it reduces travel time and logistical challenges, particularly for out-of-town attendees. Assess the availability of transportation options to and from the venue and provide information on shuttle services, nearby taxi stands, or rideshare options to help guests plan their transportation effectively.

Sustainability Considerations

Sustainability is increasingly becoming a priority for couples planning their weddings. Evaluate the venue's environmental practices and policies, looking for initiatives such as energy-efficient lighting, recycling programs, and eco-friendly catering options. Consider venues that incorporate natural elements and green spaces, promoting an eco-friendly atmosphere with lush gardens or sustainable building practices.

Venue-Specific Permits and Activities

Couples should consider venue-specific permits and requirements for activities when deciding on a venue. Public spaces often require permits regulating guest count, noise levels, and activities, which must be applied for in advance. Private properties may also need permits for noise and temporary structures. Activities such as serving alcohol and amplified music may require special permits with specific regulations. Ensuring compliance avoids legal issues and ensures a smooth event.

Health, Safety and Legal Compliance

Health and safety regulations are crucial, particularly for food service and fire safety. Catering must comply with health regulations, requiring permits, inspections, and certifications. Fire safety regulations may restrict open flames and require fire safety measures. Legal compliance includes vendor liability insurance and adherence to zoning laws affecting event size and type. **PermitZone** and **CityGrows** help identify and obtain necessary permits, streamlining the process and ensuring all legal requirements are met.

With an understanding of the key features to consider, let's move on to how AI tools can assist in comparing amenities to help you make the best choice for your wedding venue.

Comparing Amenities with AI Tools

Wedding Spot input your budget and preferences to get a list of venues with detailed cost breakdowns and transparent pricing.

VenueFinder provides a curated list of venues that match your style, budget, and other preferences.

Modsy offers 3D renderings of venues with different decor options to visualize the space.

Trustpilot allows users to browse and read reviews specifically for wedding vendors, venues, and other services. It offers user-friendly access to real customer feedback, which can help you gauge the reputation, ambiance, and overall experience of wedding-related services based on genuine reviews.

With AI tools simplifying the comparison of amenities, let's now delve into understanding pricing structures to ensure your chosen venue fits within your budget.

Understanding Pricing Structures

When searching for your wedding venue, consider the base rental fee, which varies based on factors like the day of the week, time of year, and event duration. Be aware of service fees and taxes, as these additional costs can significantly impact your budget; service fees often cover staffing, cleaning, and maintenance, while taxes are applied to the total bill. Additionally, be mindful of overtime charges, which are extra fees incurred if your event extends beyond the contracted time, to avoid any surprise costs.

In-House Services vs. External Vendors

Venues may offer bundled packages that include catering, decor, and other services. Compare these costs against hiring external vendors to determine the most cost-effective option.

Hidden Costs to Watch For

When planning your wedding, be mindful of additional costs such as corkage fees if you bring your own alcohol, which can be substantial. Also, consider setup and breakdown fees, which include labor charges for arranging and dismantling the event space. Be sure to understand the terms and conditions for security deposits, including the criteria for their return.

Platforms like **Wedding Spot** provide comprehensive cost breakdowns for various venues, allowing you to see the total estimated cost, including hidden fees and additional expenses. This transparency helps in making informed decisions and accurate budget planning.

After grasping the pricing structures, the next crucial step is negotiating contracts to secure the best terms and conditions for your chosen venue.

Understanding Contracts

Understanding contracts when booking a venue is crucial to avoid unexpected costs and ensure all your needs are met.

Typical Components of a Venue Contract: A venue contract outlines the terms and conditions of renting the venue for your wedding. Understanding these components is essential before entering negotiations.

Deposit Requirements: Clarify the amount of deposit required to secure the venue and the deadline for payment. Negotiate flexibility in deposit amounts or payment schedules.

Cancellation Policies: Review cancellation terms, including penalties for canceling or rescheduling the event. Negotiate for reasonable terms that consider unforeseen circumstances.

Terms of Service: Understand the venue's rules and regulations regarding setup, teardown, noise restrictions, and any other operational guidelines that may affect your event.

Tools like **LegalZoom** or **Rocket Lawyer** can assist in reviewing contracts, highlighting areas that may need clarification or negotiation. These tools help ensure you fully understand the terms and avoid potential pitfalls.

With a clear understanding of contracts, let's now discuss how far in advance you should book your wedding venue to ensure availability and avoid last-minute stress.

Negotiating Contracts

Effective negotiation is crucial for securing the best terms and value for your wedding venue. By being well-prepared and strategic, you can ensure that the contract meets your needs and budget while avoiding potential pitfalls.

Understanding Your Priorities: Before entering negotiations, clearly define your priorities and must-haves. Understanding what is non-negotiable and where you have flexibility can guide your discussions and help you focus on getting the most critical elements included in the contract.

Researching Venue Market Rates: Gain a thorough understanding of the average costs for similar venues in your desired location. This knowledge provides a benchmark for negotiations and helps you recognize a fair deal.

Identifying Potential Bargaining Points: Consider what aspects of the venue agreement you might be able to negotiate. Common areas for negotiation include:

Rental Fees: Ask if there's flexibility on the base rental fee, especially for off-peak dates or longer rental periods.

Package Inclusions: Request additional services or amenities to be included at no extra cost, such as extra decor items or extended access times.

Payment Terms: Negotiate for favorable payment terms, such as lower deposits, extended payment schedules, or the option to pay in installments.

Using Online Tools for Comparison

Tools like **Wedding Spot** and **VenueFinder** allow you to compare venue costs and inclusions side-by-side, providing a clear picture of what's included in each package and where there may be room for negotiation.

Effective Negotiation Strategies

Approach negotiations with a collaborative mindset rather than a confrontational one. Establishing a positive rapport with venue coordinators can lead to more favorable terms and a willingness to accommodate special requests. Be open to compromise and flexible in your demands; if the venue is firm on rental costs, they may be willing to include additional services or amenities at no extra charge.

Use competitive offers as leverage in your negotiations by sharing that you're considering other venues, which can encourage the venue to offer better terms to secure your booking. Ensure all agreed-upon terms, including negotiated discounts, added amenities, and payment schedules are documented in writing to protect both parties. Before finalizing the contract, request a detailed walkthrough of the venue with the coordinator to confirm it meets all your requirements and avoid any surprises.

Negotiating Tips

Negotiating with venues can be strategic and rewarding. To negotiate effectively, inquire about discounts for booking during off-peak months or weekdays when venues are less likely to be booked. Ask if the venue offers bundled packages that include catering, decor, or other services at a discounted rate compared to booking them separately. Negotiate flexibility on minimum spend requirements, especially if you want to customize your wedding experience rather than stick to preset packages.

Additionally, request extra perks like extended venue hours, complimentary upgrades, or added decor items, as demonstrating your commitment to booking at their venue can often lead to concessions.

Let us now look at understanding contracts to ensure you secure the best terms and conditions for your chosen venue.

How Far in Advance to Book Your Wedding Venue

Booking your wedding venue should ideally be one of the first steps in your planning process. It's recommended to secure your venue at least 12 to 18 months in advance, especially if you have a specific date in mind or if you're planning to get married during peak wedding season. Early booking ensures you have a wider selection of venues to choose from and can help you lock in your preferred date, giving you ample time to coordinate other aspects of your wedding seamlessly.

AI platforms like **VenueScanner** and **WeddingWire** help identify venue availability, compare prices, and predict future trends. These tools enable quicker comparisons and decision-making, helping you secure your preferred venue more efficiently.

With a clear understanding of how far in advance to book your wedding venue, let's now look at an example timeline to guide you through the booking process effectively.

Timeline for Booking a Wedding Venue

18-12 Months Before Wedding

Initial Research:

Begin researching potential wedding venues based on budget, location preferences, and guest capacity.

Utilize **WeddingWire** and **The Knot** to browse through a wide selection of venues, filtering by criteria such as location, price range, and style preferences.

AI-driven recommendation engines on platforms like **Zola** can suggest venues based on past preferences and wedding themes.

Virtual Tours and Initial Screening:

Take virtual tours of shortlisted venues using AI-powered virtual reality (VR) tools offered by platforms like **WeddingWire**. VR tours provide immersive experiences, allowing you to explore venue layouts and visualize wedding setups remotely.

Use AI chatbots on venue websites or platforms like **VenueScanner** to ask preliminary questions about availability, pricing, and venue policies.

12-10 Months Before Wedding

Site Visits:

Schedule in-person site visits to top venue choices. AI tools can help optimize your visit schedule based on geographic proximity and availability.

During visits, use smartphone apps with augmented reality (AR) features to visualize wedding decorations and seating arrangements in real-time at the venue. Apps like **Planit Wed** can overlay digital layouts onto physical spaces.

Budget Planning and Negotiations:

Analyze pricing trends using AI tools such as **WeddingWire** to understand typical costs for venues in your preferred location and season.

Use AI analytics to compare pricing quotes from multiple venues and negotiate effectively. AI platforms can identify cost-saving opportunities and suggest negotiation tactics based on historical data.

10-8 Months Before Wedding

Finalizing Contracts:

Narrow down your venue choices and request detailed proposals from finalists.

Utilize AI contract review tools, such as **LawGeex**, to analyze contract terms and ensure legal compliance. These tools use machine learning algorithms to identify potential risks and discrepancies in contracts.

Securing the Venue:

Sign contracts with your chosen venue and make the initial deposit to secure your wedding date.

AI tools like **VenueScanner** can monitor venue availability in real-time and alert you to any cancellations or newly available dates that may better suit your schedule.

Following this structured timeline ensures you effectively utilize AI tools and technology to streamline your venue booking process, making it efficient and stress-free.

In conclusion, selecting the perfect venue is a crucial step in wedding planning and leveraging modern technology, such as AI-powered tools and virtual tours, can simplify and enhance the venue selection process, saving time and effort while ensuring you find a location that aligns with your vision and budget.

By using AI-driven recommendations, you can receive personalized suggestions based on your specific criteria, making it easier to find venues that meet your needs. Virtual tours provide an immersive way to explore potential venues without the need for extensive travel, offering flexibility and convenience, particularly for destination weddings.

Key considerations, such as booking timelines, style, ambiance, seasonal suitability, capacity, layout, services, amenities, location, sustainability, and legal compliance, are essential to ensure your chosen venue is the right fit for your special day. AI tools can assist in evaluating these factors, providing real-time data and insights to support informed decision-making.

Negotiating contracts effectively and understanding pricing structures, including hidden costs, can help you secure the best terms and avoid unexpected expenses. Utilizing online tools for comparison and legal review ensures you are well-prepared and protected throughout the process.

Combining traditional venue selection methods with cutting-edge technology can elevate your wedding planning experience, making it more efficient, enjoyable, and tailored to your unique vision.

Embrace these modern tools to find the perfect spot that will set the tone for an extraordinary celebration.

Alicia Hernandez-Whyle

Chapter Five

Streamlining Vendor Coordination with AI

Planning a wedding is a complex process, with vendor coordination being one of the most essential elements. The success of your wedding day hinges on the seamless collaboration between various vendors, such as caterers, photographers, florists, and entertainment providers. Effective vendor coordination ensures that every detail aligns perfectly, creating a cohesive and memorable event.

However, managing multiple vendors can be overwhelming and time-consuming, often leading to stress and potential miscommunication.

Traditionally, wedding planners and brides have relied on spreadsheets, countless emails, phone calls, and in-person meetings to manage their vendor relationships. This manual approach consumes valuable time and increases the risk of errors and misaligned expectations. The intricacies involved in vendor management can be daunting, from negotiating contracts and handling payments to ensuring each vendor understands and executes your vision flawlessly. The sheer volume of tasks can often detract from the joy of planning your special day.

AI is a game-changer in the wedding planning industry. AI-driven platforms and tools offer innovative solutions to simplify vendor selection and streamline communication. These technologies harness the power of machine learning and data analytics to offer personalized recommendations, transforming vendor coordination into a seamless experience. AI can intelligently match you with vendors who best fit your criteria, preferences, and budget, saving you hours of research and reducing the risk of choosing an incompatible vendor.

This chapter explores how AI can transform vendor selection and coordination, making the process more efficient, organized, and stress-free. Embracing AI in vendor coordination not only streamlines the process but also elevates the overall quality of your wedding, allowing you to focus on celebrating your love and creating cherished memories.

To begin, it is essential to start with the foundation: identifying your vendor needs and booking the right professionals.

Section 1: Choosing and Booking Vendors

Identifying your vendor needs is the first step in ensuring a smooth wedding planning process. Begin by thoroughly assessing your wedding requirements, considering essential services such as catering, photography, floral arrangements, entertainment, and more. Reflect on your wedding style, budget, and personal preferences to determine which vendors are necessary to bring your vision to life. Creating a comprehensive list of desired services will help you stay organized and focused throughout the planning process.

When detailing your needs, consider the specific qualities and attributes you seek in each vendor, such as their experience, style, availability, and compatibility with your wedding theme. This preparation not only streamlines the vendor selection process but also helps you communicate your expectations clearly to potential vendors. By knowing exactly what you need and want, you can ensure that you find professionals who align perfectly with your wedding goals, making the planning process more efficient and enjoyable.

AI-Driven Vendor Platforms

AI-driven vendor platforms have revolutionized the wedding planning process, offering efficient and tailored solutions for vendor management. Top platforms like **WedMatch, Zola,** and **WeddingWire** provide comprehensive tools to streamline your vendor selection.

WedMatch uses advanced algorithms to match you with vendors based on your specific preferences and budget, ensuring a perfect fit.

Zola offers an all-in-one wedding planning experience with personalized vendor recommendations and a centralized dashboard for easy management.

WeddingWire boasts an extensive vendor database and AI-powered search capabilities, making it simple to find and book the ideal vendors. These platforms save time, reduce stress, and ensure compatibility with your vision. Brides who have used these

AI-driven platforms report higher satisfaction and a smoother planning experience. For instance, Naomi, a recent bride, found her dream photographer and florist through WedMatch, praising the platform's accuracy and ease of use.

Vendor Matching Algorithms

AI algorithms match you with the best vendors based on your specific preferences and budget. These algorithms analyze your input criteria, such as wedding style, location, budget, and specific needs, and then cross-reference this information with a vast database of vendors. By considering factors like vendor experience, style compatibility, and user reviews, the AI can provide you with a curated list of vendors that perfectly align with your vision. This approach ensures a seamless vendor selection process, making your wedding planning more enjoyable and efficient.

To utilize these algorithms, follow this step-by-step guide:

Step 1: Choose an AI Vendor Platform: Select a reputable platform like **WedMatch, Zola,** or **WeddingWire.**

Step 2: Create an Account: Sign up and create a profile with basic wedding details.

Step 3: Input Wedding Details: Enter information about your wedding date, location, and guest count.

Step 4: Set Your Budget: Specify your overall budget and allocate amounts for different vendor categories.

Step 5: Define Preferences: Indicate your preferences for vendor style, experience level, and any special requirements.

Step 6: Review Recommendations: The AI will generate a list of vendors that match your criteria. Review and compare these recommendations.

Step 7: Contact Vendors: Reach out to your top choices directly through the platform to start discussions and negotiations.

By following these steps, you can leverage AI to find the best vendors efficiently and effectively.

Once you've selected your vendors, the next step is ensuring effective communication to keep everyone aligned and on track.

Alicia Hernandez-Whyle

Section 2: Communicating with Vendors

AI chatbots and automated reminders are invaluable for maintaining effective communication with your wedding vendors. Setting up AI chatbots for initial vendor inquiries can streamline the process, providing instant responses and gathering essential information. Platforms like Zola and WeddingWire offer chatbot features that can be easily customized to handle inquiries, check availability, and provide pricing details. This automation ensures that you receive timely responses without the need for constant manual follow-up.

Customizing automated reminders for follow-ups and deadlines is equally important. AI tools can send reminders for upcoming meetings, payment deadlines, and contract reviews, helping you stay organized and on track. For instance, you can set reminders for key milestones like payment due dates, finalizing contracts, and confirming details with vendors. These reminders ensure that no critical tasks are overlooked, reducing the risk of last-minute issues.

By leveraging AI chatbots and automated reminders, you can ensure smooth, efficient communication with your vendors, allowing you to focus on other aspects of your wedding planning.

Centralized Communication Hubs

Utilizing AI-driven communication hubs to keep all vendor correspondence in one place is a game-changer for wedding planning. Platforms like Trello, Slack, and Asana integrate AI to centralize your communication, allowing you to manage all interactions with vendors efficiently. These hubs consolidate emails, messages, and documents, providing a single point of access for all your planning needs. By organizing all your vendor interactions in one location, you can easily track conversations, share updates, and ensure everyone is on the same page.

The benefits of having a centralized system for tracking conversations and documents are significant. Firstly, it reduces the risk of miscommunication by ensuring that all parties have access to the same information. You can maintain a clear record of agreements, timelines, and changes, which is crucial for accountability and reference.

Secondly, it saves time by streamlining your workflow; you no longer need to search through scattered emails or files to find important details.

Lastly, it enhances collaboration by allowing real-time updates and feedback, ensuring a smoother planning process. By implementing a centralized communication hub, you can significantly improve the efficiency and effectiveness of your vendor management.

Real-Time Language Translation

Leveraging AI translation tools for communicating with vendors who speak different languages can be a vital asset in wedding planning, especially for destination weddings or multicultural teams. Tools like **Google Translate**, **DeepL**, and **Microsoft Translator** offer real-time translation services, allowing seamless conversations with vendors. These AI-driven tools can translate written messages and spoken conversations, ensuring clear and efficient communication.

Ensuring accurate communication across language barriers is crucial to avoid misunderstandings and ensure that your wedding plans are executed flawlessly. AI translation tools help bridge the gap, providing precise translations that capture the nuances of your requirements and the vendor's responses. This not only facilitates smooth communication but also builds trust and rapport with your vendors. By using these tools, you can confidently engage with a diverse range of vendors, knowing that language differences will not hinder the success of your wedding planning.

After establishing clear communication, the next crucial step is finalizing contracts and ensuring all agreements are securely in place.

Section 3: Finalizing Contracts

Handling contracts and payments efficiently is crucial in the wedding planning process, and AI tools can significantly enhance this aspect. Secure and efficient financial transactions are made possible with AI assistance, ensuring that payments to vendors are processed seamlessly and on time. Platforms like **HoneyBook** and **Zoho** Contracts provide secure payment gateways that protect your financial information and reduce the risk of fraud.

Automating contract generation and signature collection simplifies the administrative burden of finalizing vendor agreements. AI tools can generate customized contracts based on your specific terms and requirements, ensuring that all legal and logistical details are covered. E-signature features allow vendors to sign contracts electronically, speeding up the process and reducing the need for physical paperwork.

Ensuring data security and compliance with AI tools is paramount. These platforms utilize advanced encryption and security protocols to protect your sensitive information. Compliance with industry standards and regulations, such as the General Data Protection Regulation, is also maintained, ensuring that your data and transactions are secure. By leveraging AI for handling contracts and payments, you can streamline these critical tasks, ensuring a smooth and secure process from start to finish.

AI-powered contract analysis is a valuable tool in wedding planning, providing a thorough review and highlighting critical contract terms and clauses. Tools like **Luminance** and **LawGeex** use machine learning algorithms to scan and analyze contracts, identifying key provisions such as payment schedules, cancellation policies, and service deliverables. This helps you fully understand the terms you are agreeing to, minimizing the chances of misunderstandings or disputes. By using AI to review contracts, you significantly reduce the risk of missing important details or hidden fees.

These tools can flag unusual or non-standard clauses that may require further attention or negotiation. Additionally, AI can compare your contract against industry standards and best practices, ensuring that you receive fair and reasonable terms. This comprehensive analysis provides peace of mind, knowing that your agreements are secure and transparent. Utilizing AI-powered contract analysis enhances your ability to manage vendor relationships effectively and ensures that all contractual obligations are clear and enforceable.

To ensure smooth financial management, let's delve into payment scheduling and tracking, and how these tools can help keep your wedding budget on track.

Payment Scheduling and Tracking

Setting up automated payment schedules and reminders is a crucial aspect of managing wedding expenses. **HoneyBook** and **Zoho** Invoice allow you to automate payment schedules, ensuring that each vendor receives timely payments according to the agreed terms. You can set up reminders for upcoming payments, which help you avoid late fees and maintain good relationships with your vendors. These reminders can be customized to alert you well in advance, giving you ample time to prepare and review your finances.

Tracking payment status and outstanding balances is made easy with AI tools. These platforms provide real-time updates on payment status, allowing you to see which payments have been made, which are pending, and which are overdue. Detailed dashboards provide a clear view of your financial commitments, making it easier to manage your budget effectively. AI-driven insights can also alert you to any discrepancies or issues, enabling you to address them promptly. By using AI for payment scheduling and tracking, you can ensure financial accuracy and maintain a stress-free planning process.

To ensure you choose the best professionals, let's explore how vendor reviews and ratings can guide your decision-making process.

Section 4: Vendor Reviews and Ratings

Using AI to aggregate and analyze vendor reviews from various platforms can significantly enhance your decision-making process. AI tools can scrape reviews from multiple sources, such as Yelp, Google, and specialized wedding sites, compiling them into a comprehensive database. This aggregation allows you to see a holistic view of each vendor's performance, providing a more reliable basis for comparison.

Identifying patterns and common feedback points is made easier with AI analysis. These tools can sift through vast amounts of data, highlighting recurring themes and sentiments in the reviews. For instance, if multiple reviews mention punctuality, quality of service, or responsiveness, the AI can pinpoint these as strengths or weaknesses. This level of insight helps you make informed choices, ensuring you select vendors who consistently meet expectations and align with your wedding vision.

By leveraging AI to analyze vendor reviews, you can gain a deeper understanding of each vendor's reputation, ultimately leading to better vendor selections and a smoother wedding planning experience. AI-generated ratings can significantly aid in making informed vendor choices. By analyzing aggregated data from reviews, performance metrics, and customer feedback, AI tools can generate comprehensive and unbiased ratings for each vendor.

These ratings provide a quick and reliable way to assess a vendor's overall quality and reliability, helping you to narrow down your options efficiently. Personalizing recommendations based on your specific needs and preferences is another powerful feature of AI. These tools can consider factors such as your wedding style, budget, location, and specific requirements to suggest vendors that best match your criteria. For instance, if you prioritize creativity in floral arrangements or punctuality in photography services, the AI can highlight vendors who excel in these areas. This personalized approach ensures that the vendors you choose are not only top-rated but also aligned with your unique vision and expectations.

Alicia Hernandez-Whyle

By embracing AI in your wedding planning journey, you can significantly reduce the time, stress, and potential errors associated with traditional vendor management. With AI-generated ratings and personalized recommendations, you can make confident and well-informed decisions, ensuring a seamless and successful vendor experience.

Part Three: Design and Personalization

Alicia Hernandez-Whyle

Chapter Six

Food and Menu Planning with AI

Food and menu planning are essential aspects of any wedding event, ensuring that guests have an enjoyable and memorable experience. A well-curated menu can enhance the celebration's ambiance, reflect the couple's personality, and cater to diverse dietary preferences and cultural traditions. The process involves careful consideration of seasonality, budget, guest preferences, and the wedding's overall theme. With the growing complexity of these tasks, couples and planners increasingly seek innovative solutions to streamline and optimize their culinary planning efforts.

AI-powered tools have revolutionized the culinary world, offering features designed to simplify and enhance the food planning process for weddings. These technologies analyze vast amounts of data to predict trends, suggest menu items, and generate customized recipes based on the couple's preferences and dietary requirements. By leveraging machine learning algorithms, AI tools provide insights into guest preferences, enabling a more personalized dining experience. Additionally, AI helps optimize costs, reduce food waste, and ensure smooth food preparation by accurately estimating quantities and sourcing ingredients. As technology evolves, AI integration in food and menu planning is becoming indispensable in the wedding industry, offering unparalleled precision and efficiency in creating unforgettable culinary experiences.

Building on this foundation, understanding AI in menu planning reveals how these advanced tools transform culinary customization and optimization.

Understanding AI in Menu Planning

AI algorithms have become a transformative force in menu planning, particularly for wedding events. These sophisticated algorithms analyze a multitude of data points, such as seasonal ingredients, dietary preferences, cultural traditions, and even the latest culinary trends. By processing this data, AI systems can suggest customized menu options that align with the couple's vision and the event's overall theme. For instance, machine learning models can predict popular dishes based on past wedding menus and guest feedback, ensuring that the food offerings are both innovative and crowd-pleasing. This level of customization was previously achievable only through extensive manual effort and expertise.

The benefits of using AI for menu planning are manifold. First and foremost, AI significantly reduces the time and effort required to create a perfect menu. Planners and couples can explore a variety of tailored menu options with just a few clicks, making it easier to experiment with different cuisines and dishes.

Moreover, AI-powered menu planning enhances the overall dining experience for wedding guests. By incorporating data on dietary restrictions and preferences, AI ensures that the menu caters to a diverse audience, offering delicious options for everyone, including those with specific dietary needs. This level of personalization extends to the presentation and pairing of dishes, where AI can suggest complementary flavors and styles, creating a cohesive and delightful dining experience.

With a grasp of AI's role in menu planning, let's now explore how AI can aid with wedding cake selection.

AI-Powered Wedding Cake Selection

Selecting the perfect wedding cake is a crucial part of wedding planning, and AI can greatly simplify this process. Tools like **Bakediary** allow couples to input their preferences for flavors, design styles, and dietary restrictions. These platforms then analyze the data, cross-referencing it with current trends and customer reviews, to suggest cake options that align with the couple's vision.

Advanced features, such as virtual 3D models provided by **CakeVR**, allow couples to visualize their cake, interact with a 3D model, and view it from various angles before making a final decision. Additionally, **FoodParing** offers real-time recommendations for flavor pairings and unique cake designs based on the wedding theme. These AI-driven tools also help identify the best local bakers who excel in the desired cake style, considering factors like location, budget, and previous customer satisfaction.

This combination of personalized recommendations and immersive visualization ensures that the wedding cake is a stunning and delicious centerpiece that perfectly complements the overall wedding theme.

Alicia Hernandez-Whyle

Analyzing Personal Tastes and Dietary Needs

Customizing a wedding menu begins with a deep understanding of the couple's personal tastes and the dietary needs of their guests. AI tools excel in this area by collecting and analyzing data from various sources, including the couple's favorite foods, past dining experiences, and guest dietary restrictions. This data-driven approach allows for the creation of a menu that is both personalized and inclusive. Whether guests require gluten-free options, vegetarian meals, or allergy-friendly dishes, AI can ensure that every dietary need is met without compromising on taste or creativity. This thoughtful customization guarantees that all guests, regardless of their dietary preferences, can enjoy the celebration to the fullest.

Integrating Cultural and Regional Food Preferences

Incorporating cultural and regional food preferences is another critical aspect of menu customization. Weddings often celebrate not just the union of two individuals but also their cultural heritages and family traditions. AI-powered menu planning tools can help seamlessly integrate these elements by suggesting traditional dishes from the couple's cultural backgrounds or popular regional specialties. By analyzing trends and recipes from various cultures, AI ensures that the menu honors these traditions while also introducing guests to new and exciting flavors. This cultural integration adds a meaningful and personal touch to the wedding feast, making it a memorable experience for everyone involved.

Ensuring Menu Variety and Balance

Achieving a balanced and varied menu is essential to cater to diverse palates and provide a well-rounded dining experience. AI can assist in creating a menu that includes a harmonious mix of appetizers, main courses, and desserts, ensuring that there is something for everyone. By evaluating the nutritional content and flavor profiles of different dishes, AI ensures that the menu is not only delicious but also balanced in terms of nutrients and taste. This balance extends to the inclusion of various textures, colors, and presentation styles, enhancing the overall dining experience. With AI's assistance, planners can create a menu that is visually appealing, nutritionally balanced, and diverse in flavors, making the wedding meal a highlight of the celebration.

Having explored how AI personalizes menu planning, let's delve into the specific tools and applications that make this technology accessible and effective for creating exceptional wedding menus.

Top AI-Powered Menu Planning Tools

In wedding planning, several AI-powered tools have emerged to streamline and improve the menu planning process. One such tool is **Tastewise**, which leverages AI to analyze global food trends and provide personalized menu suggestions based on current culinary preferences. Another popular tool is **MeazureUp**, designed to optimize restaurant and catering operations by offering insights into menu performance and guest preferences. **FoodPairing** is another innovative application that uses AI to suggest complementary flavors and ingredients, ensuring a harmonious and delicious menu. These tools not only simplify the planning process but also offer unique features that cater to the specific needs of wedding events.

Guide on Using Tastewise

To utilize **Tastewise** for your wedding menu planning, start by creating an account and inputting basic information about your event, such as the number of guests, dietary restrictions, and preferred cuisines. The AI will then analyze this data alongside global food trends to generate a variety of menu options. You can further refine these suggestions by selecting specific dishes, ingredients, or themes that resonate with your vision. **Tastewise's** intuitive interface allows you to adjust the menu in real time, ensuring it aligns perfectly with your preferences. Once the menu is finalized, you can use the platform's features to source ingredients and connect with local vendors, streamlining the entire process from planning to execution.

Guide on Using FoodPairing

Using **FoodPairing** starts with registering on their platform and entering details about your wedding event and culinary preferences. Begin by specifying key ingredients or dishes you want to include in your menu. The AI will then analyze these inputs and suggest complementary flavors and ingredients that enhance the overall taste profile. This tool is particularly useful for creating unique and innovative dishes that surprise and delight your guests. As you explore the suggested pairings, you can experiment with different combinations and view detailed recipes.

FoodPairing also provides insights into presentation and plating, helping you create a visually stunning and cohesive menu. With its advanced AI capabilities, FoodPairing ensures that every dish is a perfect match, making your wedding feast truly memorable.

Transitioning from the tools and applications available, the next crucial step involves finding and working with caterers to bring your personalized menu to life.

AI for Caterer Selection

Alicia Hernandez-Whyle

Choosing the right catering service is crucial for the success of any wedding event. AI technology offers a sophisticated approach to this selection process by evaluating a wide range of criteria to identify the best caterers for your specific needs. Key criteria include the caterer's experience with weddings, their ability to accommodate dietary restrictions, the variety and quality of their menu options, and their reputation for reliability and professionalism. By analyzing these factors, AI tools can provide a shortlist of top candidates, ensuring you have access to the best possible services for your special day.

Criteria for Selecting the Best Catering Services

When selecting a catering service, it's important to consider several key factors to ensure a seamless and enjoyable dining experience for your guests. First, evaluate the caterer's experience with weddings and their ability to deliver large-scale events. Next, consider their menu options and flexibility in accommodating dietary restrictions and preferences. Additionally, assess their reputation through reviews and testimonials, focusing on their reliability, quality of service, and responsiveness. Finally, consider their pricing and ability to work within your budget without compromising on quality. AI tools can simplify this process by gathering and analyzing the data to deliver a thorough assessment of each caterer.

AI for Comparing Caterer Review and Portfolios

AI-powered platforms such as **WeddingWire** leverage machine learning algorithms to compare caterer reviews, ratings, and portfolios efficiently. These tools aggregate data from multiple sources, including online reviews, social media feedback, and professional ratings, to provide a holistic view of each caterer's performance. By inputting your specific requirements, the AI can filter through hundreds of caterers, highlighting those with the highest ratings and most positive feedback.

Additionally, these platforms often feature detailed portfolios showcasing past events, allowing you to assess the caterer's style and capabilities visually. This comprehensive analysis helps you make an informed decision, ensuring that the caterer you choose aligns perfectly with your wedding vision and expectations.

Utilizing AI for Efficient Communication with Caterers

Efficient communication with caterers is essential to ensure that all details are aligned and the event runs smoothly. AI-powered platforms such as **Slack** and **Trello** offer robust solutions for streamlining communication and coordination with catering services. These tools can automate routine interactions, such as confirming details, sharing updates, and coordinating schedules. AI chatbots can manage initial inquiries and offer immediate answers to frequently asked questions, freeing up time for more personalized interactions.

Additionally, AI can help track all communication threads, ensuring that nothing falls through the cracks and that all stakeholders are kept in the loop. This organized and responsive communication flow helps build a strong working relationship with your caterer, ensuring clarity and efficiency throughout the planning process.

Scheduling Tastings and Meetings through AI Tools

AI tools like **Calendly** and **Doodle** can significantly simplify the process of scheduling tastings and meetings with caterers. These platforms allow you to set your availability preferences and automatically coordinate with the caterer's schedule to find mutually convenient times for appointments. By eliminating the back and forth typically involved in scheduling, AI tools ensure that tastings and meetings are arranged quickly and efficiently.

Furthermore, these platforms can send automated reminders and updates, helping to keep both parties informed and reducing the risk of missed appointments. By leveraging AI for scheduling, you can focus more on the creative aspects of menu planning, confident that the logistical details are being handled seamlessly.

Building on efficient communication, effective contract management is essential to solidify agreements and ensure all details are meticulously handled.

AI Assistance in Reviewing and Finalizing Contracts

Navigating the complexities of catering contracts can be daunting, but AI-powered tools offer valuable assistance in reviewing and finalizing these agreements. Platforms like **DocuSign** and **LawGeex** utilize advanced algorithms to analyze contract terms and highlight critical clauses, such as payment schedules, cancellation policies, and service guarantees. These tools can quickly identify any discrepancies or unfavorable terms, ensuring that you are fully informed before signing. By automating the review process, AI can significantly reduce the time and effort required to scrutinize lengthy legal documents, helping you to avoid potential pitfalls and secure a fair and transparent agreement.

Additionally, AI can assist in the negotiation phase by providing data-driven insights and suggestions for contract modifications. Tools like **PactSafe** can track contract versions, facilitate collaborative edits, and ensure that all changes are documented accurately. This level of oversight and precision helps to streamline the finalization process, making it easier to reach mutually agreeable terms with your caterer. With AI's support, you can confidently manage your catering contracts, knowing that every detail has been thoroughly vetted and addressed, ultimately contributing to a smoother and more successful wedding planning experience.

With contracts in place, the focus shifts to creating unique dining experiences that leave a lasting impression on your guests.

Creating Unique Dining Experiences

Designing theme-based menus with the help of AI can transform your wedding reception into a truly unforgettable event. AI tools like **Chef Watson** by IBM can analyze your chosen theme and suggest creative menu options that align perfectly with the overall aesthetic and mood of your celebration. Whether you're aiming for a rustic, elegant, or avant-garde dining experience, AI can recommend dishes, ingredients, and presentations that encapsulate your vision. By leveraging vast databases of recipes and culinary trends, these tools can craft a cohesive and innovative menu that surprises and delights your guests, ensuring that every meal reflects the unique personality and style of your wedding.

Incorporating Guest Preferences and Dietary Restrictions

AI technology excels at personalizing dining experiences by incorporating guest preferences and dietary restrictions into the menu planning process. Tools like **Spoon Guru** can collect and analyze data on your guests' dietary needs, such as allergies, vegetarian or vegan preferences, and other specific requirements. By integrating this information, AI can suggest menu items that accommodate all guests, ensuring that everyone can enjoy the meal without worry.

Furthermore, AI can provide alternative ingredient suggestions and recipe modifications to create inclusive dishes that maintain their flavor and appeal. This attention to detail ensures a seamless dining experience that respects and celebrates the diverse tastes and needs of your wedding attendees.

Examining real-world applications, let's look at examples of weddings with successful personalized culinary experiences to understand the impact of thoughtful menu customization.

Real Bride Experience

One notable example of a wedding with a successful personalized culinary experience is the wedding of Emily and Mark, who utilized AI to create a themed menu that reflected their shared love of Italian cuisine. Using the **TasteWise** AI platform, they designed a bespoke menu that included unique twists on classic Italian dishes, such as truffle-infused risotto and deconstructed tiramisu. The AI also helped incorporate the couple's favorite local ingredients, ensuring that each dish was both personal and exceptional.

Another case is the wedding of Savita and Singh, who prioritized accommodating their guests' diverse dietary needs. By leveraging the **Spoon Guru** AI tool, they crafted a menu that included vegan, gluten-free, and nut-free options without compromising on flavor or variety. The AI provided alternative ingredient suggestions and recipe adjustments, resulting in a harmonious and inclusive dining experience that all guests could enjoy.

These case studies illustrate how AI can be leveraged to create memorable, personalized culinary experiences that cater to diverse tastes and preferences.

Transitioning to sustainability, let's explore the environmental benefits of eco-friendly catering and how it contributes to a greener wedding celebration.

Environmental Benefits of Eco-Friendly Catering

Choosing eco-friendly catering options for your wedding significantly reduces the environmental impact of the event. Sustainable food choices often involve sourcing ingredients from local, organic farms, which reduces the carbon footprint associated with transportation and supports regional agriculture. Additionally, eco-friendly catering emphasizes the use of seasonal produce, minimizing the need for energy-intensive storage and transportation. These practices contribute to a reduction in greenhouse gas emissions, soil degradation, and water pollution, promoting a healthier planet.

Health Benefits of Sustainable Food Options

Sustainable food choices also offer numerous health benefits for you and your guests. Organic and locally sourced foods tend to be fresher and richer in nutrients compared to conventionally produced alternatives. By avoiding the use of synthetic pesticides and fertilizers, these foods are less likely to contain harmful chemicals, making them safer for consumption. Additionally, sustainable menus often emphasize whole, minimally processed foods, which can lead to improved digestion, better overall health, and enhanced well-being for everyone at your wedding.

Finding Local and Organic Food Suppliers Using AI

AI technology can be instrumental in identifying and sourcing local and organic food suppliers. Platforms like **Sustainable Food Trust** and **Locavore** utilize AI algorithms to map out regional suppliers that adhere to sustainable practices. These tools analyze various factors such as proximity, certification standards, and supplier reviews to provide a curated list of eco-friendly vendors. By leveraging AI, couples can ensure that their wedding menu supports local farmers and promotes sustainable agricultural practices, contributing to a more environmentally conscious celebration.

AI for Seasonal Plant-Based Menus

AI can also assist in designing menus that emphasize seasonal and plant-based ingredients, which are often more sustainable. Tools like **PlantJammer** and **EcoMenu** use AI to suggest dishes based on the availability of seasonal produce and the couple's dietary preferences. These platforms can recommend innovative plant-based recipes that reduce reliance on resource-intensive animal products, thereby lowering the event's overall carbon footprint. By following AI-driven recommendations, couples can create delicious, eco-friendly menus that are both sustainable and health-conscious.

To complement the environmental benefits of eco-friendly catering, implementing waste reduction strategies is essential for creating a sustainable and responsible wedding event.

AI for Portion Sizes and Reducing Waste

AI tools such as **LeanPath** and **Winnow** can play a crucial role in minimizing food waste at weddings. These platforms use AI to analyze guest lists and consumption patterns to accurately estimate portion sizes, ensuring that food is neither overprepared nor underutilized. By providing precise portion control recommendations, these tools help caterers prepare the right amount of food, significantly reducing the amount of waste generated.

Additionally, AI-powered tools like **Leanpath** can monitor food waste throughout the event, providing real-time insights and adjustments to optimize food usage. **Leanpath** uses smart scales, cameras, and advanced algorithms to track waste, identify patterns, and suggest actionable strategies to reduce excess, ensuring a more sustainable and efficient event.

Partnering for Food Donations and Composting

To address any unavoidable food surplus, couples can partner with organizations like **Food Rescue US** and **CompostNow** for food donations and composting. These organizations often use AI to coordinate the collection and distribution of excess food to local shelters and food banks, ensuring that leftover meals benefit those in need rather than ending up in landfills.

In conclusion, incorporating AI-powered tools into food and menu planning for weddings offers a multitude of benefits, from personalized culinary experiences to enhanced sustainability. By leveraging AI to analyze data on guest preferences, dietary needs, and cultural traditions, couples can create customized menus that delight and cater to all attendees. AI's ability to streamline communication with caterers, optimize ingredient procurement, and manage contracts ensures a seamless planning process, allowing couples to focus on enjoying their special day.

Chapter Seven

Curating Your Wedding Style with AI

As the wedding industry evolves, the role of artificial intelligence (AI) has become increasingly essential in transforming how couples plan their big day. Previously, we explored how AI assists in various aspects of wedding planning, from menu planning to finding the perfect vendors.

In this chapter, we turn our focus on selecting wedding style and design, where AI's innovative capabilities offer brides and grooms a wealth of personalized options.

Join us as we explore how AI can guide you through the process of defining and refining your wedding style. From mood boards and color palettes to dress selections and decor themes, we'll uncover how AI is revolutionizing wedding design, making it more accessible, customizable, and ultimately, a reflection of who you are as a couple.

Design Inspiration through AI Tools

AI-powered image recognition is revolutionizing how brides source and organize design inspiration for their weddings. By harnessing advanced AI tools, users can effortlessly scan platforms like **Pinterest, Instagram**, and various wedding blogs to gather a vast array of creative ideas. These tools utilize sophisticated algorithms to recognize patterns, themes, and visual elements that align with the user's preferences. For instance, a bride might upload a few images of her favorite wedding décor, and the AI system will analyze these to suggest similar designs, color palettes, and themes from across the web. This technology not only saves time but also ensures a cohesive and personalized wedding aesthetic.

Additionally, AI-powered image recognition can categorize and organize these inspirations into mood boards or digital scrapbooks, making it easier for brides to visualize their big day.

Virtual mood boards take this a step further by using AI platforms to compile collected ideas into a unified vision. These platforms can seamlessly integrate various elements, allowing brides to see how different components work together, ensuring a harmonious and well-coordinated wedding design.

By streamlining the discovery and organization process, AI tools empower brides to make informed decisions and collaborate more effectively with vendors and planners. As a result, the integration of AI in wedding planning offers brides an innovative way to bring their dream weddings to life with precision and creativity.

Building on the design inspiration provided by AI tools, let's explore how these tools create personalized mood boards and style suggestions.

Personalized Mood Boards and Style Suggestions

AI tools like **Pinterest** offer powerful customization features that enable brides to create personalized mood boards and style suggestions tailored to their unique tastes and wedding visions. By leveraging advanced algorithms, **Pinterest** analyzes user preferences such as color schemes, themes, and specific design elements to compile individualized mood boards. Brides can input their favorite styles, upload inspiration images, and select specific wedding themes. This level of personalization ensures every aspect of the wedding is in harmony, creating a seamless and well-coordinated event.

Integrating personal preferences further enhances the customization process. AI algorithms analyze individual tastes, venue details, and seasonal trends to recommend suitable wedding styles. For instance, if a bride chooses a historic venue for her vintage-themed wedding, the AI can suggest décor elements and attire that complement the setting. Additionally, by considering seasonal trends, the AI ensures the suggestions are current and relevant, incorporating the latest in wedding fashion and design. Collaborative AI-driven platforms elevate these features by allowing couples and planners to design and refine wedding styles interactively.

With real-time updates and shared access, everyone involved can contribute ideas, make adjustments, and see instant visualizations of changes. This collaborative approach fosters better communication and ensures the wedding design reflects the couple's vision, seamlessly integrating input from all stakeholders.

Next, we transition from AI-driven style suggestions to finding the perfect balance between trends and personal taste.

Balancing Trends with Personal Taste

Minted is transforming the wedding planning field by providing sophisticated tools for balancing trends with personal taste. One of its key features is trend analysis, where **Minted** scans sources like social media, wedding blogs, and fashion sites to identify current wedding trends. These trends can range from popular color schemes and décor styles to favored dress designs and floral arrangements. The AI then suggests ways to incorporate these trends into a wedding plan while maintaining the couple's unique style.

For example, if a couple loves a classic theme but wants to include contemporary elements, **Minted** can recommend modern touches that enhance rather than overshadow the traditional aspects. This might include suggesting a trending color palette that complements the classic décor or proposing the latest floral arrangement styles that match the overall aesthetic. Additionally, **Minted** provides insights into seasonal trends, ensuring that the suggestions are both stylish and seasonally appropriate.

Advanced personalization algorithms play a crucial role in this process. These algorithms analyze the couple's preferences, such as favorite colors, themes, and design elements, and blend these with identified trends. This ensures a cohesive and personalized wedding design, seamlessly integrating the couple's vision with contemporary trends.`

Chloe and Isaac's Wedding: Merging Trends with Personal Tastes via AI

For their wedding, Chloe and Isaac envisioned floral arrangements that would not only be trendy but also deeply reflective of their unique style and personalities. Chloe had always dreamed of a wedding where the flowers would evoke a sense of romance and elegance yet still feel fresh and modern. However, the sheer variety of choices available left her feeling overwhelmed and unsure of how to bring her vision to life. While researching floral design options online, she stumbled upon **Bloomerent** AI, a cutting-edge floral design tool that promised to simplify the process and deliver personalized results.

Intrigued by the possibilities, Chloe decided to give **Bloomerent** AI a try. The tool allowed her and Isaac to input their preferences: deep burgundy, blush pink, and soft ivory for colors, and peonies, garden roses, and dahlias as their favorite flowers. The AI analyzed current wedding floral trends, noting the popularity of pampas grass, eucalyptus, and muted color palettes.

One of the standout features of **Bloomerent** AI was its ability to recommend specific floral arrangements based on their inputs. To blend trends with their personal tastes, the AI suggested bouquets featuring Chloe's favorite blush pink peonies, accented with garden roses and dahlias. To incorporate trendy elements, the bouquets included pampas grass and eucalyptus, providing a modern touch. The centerpieces mirrored this blend, combining the trendy muted color palette with vibrant flowers and rustic elements like burlap-wrapped vases and wooden accents. With the AI's suggestions in hand, Chloe was able to work with a local florist who brought the digital vision to life with stunning precision.

When the big day arrived, Chloe was overjoyed with the final result. The floral arrangements were everything she had hoped for: beautiful, cohesive, and uniquely theirs. The sight of the flowers, thoughtfully arranged and perfectly aligned with their vision, filled her with a deep sense of satisfaction.

This seamless integration not only impressed their guests but also ensured that Chloe and Isaac's wedding decor felt deeply personal and on-trend.

Now, we explore how to make informed decisions when choosing between handling tasks yourself or hiring professional help.

Alicia Hernandez-Whyle

DIY vs. Professional Help

Planning your wedding can be one of the most rewarding and challenging experiences of your life. You are likely filled with excitement about crafting a day that reflects your love story, but also faced with the practical realities of managing a budget, timeline, and myriad details. The question of whether to take on the planning yourself or seek professional help is a significant one, influenced by your budget, time, and personal preferences.

Beyond these considerations, the decision also hinges on your level of comfort with the planning process. If you thrive on organization and enjoy coordinating details, DIY planning with the help of AI tools might be perfect for you. However, if you find the process overwhelming or have a particularly complex vision for your wedding, professional planners can offer invaluable expertise and peace of mind, ensuring every detail is flawlessly executed.

While DIY planning can be rewarding, knowing when to seek professional help can save time, stress, and money. Understanding when to bring in experts is key to a successful and enjoyable planning experience.

When to Consider Professional Help

Planning a wedding involves numerous decisions, and knowing when to seek professional help can make all the difference.

Complexity: If your wedding involves intricate details, such as coordinating multiple vendors, managing a large guest list, or planning destination logistics, professional help is invaluable. Wedding planners have the expertise to handle complex logistics and ensure that everything runs smoothly on your big day.

Time Constraints: Balancing wedding planning with a demanding career or personal life can be difficult. If the volume of tasks becomes overwhelming, hiring a professional can help you manage your time more effectively. They can handle the details, allowing you to enjoy the lead-up to your wedding.

Cost Considerations: Understanding the budget implications of DIY versus professional assistance is crucial. DIY planning can seem more budget-friendly, especially with the help of AI tools that offer detailed budgeting assistance and affordable options for venues, vendors and decor. However, professional planners often secure better rates and exclusive deals, making their services cost-effective in the long run.

The decision between DIY and professional help doesn't have to be all-or-nothing. A hybrid approach, combining the personal touch of DIY with professional expertise, often works best. This strategy ensures a beautiful, memorable day without unnecessary financial stress, balancing personal involvement with expert guidance.

As we move forward, let's examine how to effectively combine DIY methods with professional help using practical tips.

Practical Tips for a Hybrid Approach:

Prioritize Tasks: Decide which aspects of your wedding you want to handle yourself and which you'd prefer to delegate to professionals.

Use AI Tools Wisely: Leverage AI tools to manage tasks like budgeting and guest lists, freeing up your time for the creative elements you enjoy.

Communicate Clearly: Work closely with wedding professionals you hire to ensure they understand your vision and can help bring it to life.

With a hybrid approach leveraging both DIY efforts supported by AI and professional expertise, you can create a wedding that is truly unique, beautifully personal, and free from the overwhelming burden of doing everything yourself.

Alicia Hernandez-Whyle

Chapter Eight

Dress to Impress: AI in Bridal Fashion

For centuries, bridal fashion has served as a profound expression of cultural traditions, personal identity, and aesthetic sensibilities. From the intricate lacework of Victorian gowns to the minimalist elegance of modern wedding dresses, the evolution of bridal fashion mirrors the shifts in societal norms and technological advancements. In this chapter, we delve into how the latest frontier of technology, artificial intelligence, is revolutionizing the bridal fashion industry, transforming the way brides select, personalize, and purchase their wedding attire.

The Tech Savvy Bride

Bridal fashion has undergone significant transformations through history, shaped by cultural traditions, economic factors, and changing aesthetic preferences. During the Renaissance, brides wore dresses that reflected their social status and wealth, often adorned with luxurious fabrics and elaborate embellishments. The iconic white wedding dress, popularized by Queen Victoria in 1840, became a symbol of purity and tradition, setting a trend that persists to this day.

The 20th century saw the democratization of bridal fashion, with mass production making elegant wedding dresses more accessible. The latter half of the century witnessed the rise of designer bridal wear, offering brides a wide range of styles and customizations. The advent of the internet in the late 1990s and early 2000s further transformed the industry, introducing online shopping and digital catalogs, which allowed brides to browse thousands of designs from the comfort of their homes.

As we enter the era of digital transformation, technology continues to play a pivotal role in shaping bridal fashion. From virtual reality (VR) fittings to 3D printing of bespoke dresses, the industry is constantly evolving to meet the demands of modern brides. However, the most significant leap forward in recent years has been the integration of artificial intelligence, which is redefining how brides approach the process of finding their perfect wedding attire.

Next, we uncover the exciting changes AI brings to bridal fashion.

The Impact of AI on Bridal Fashion

Artificial intelligence is set to revolutionize the bridal fashion industry, bringing numerous benefits that enhance and simplify the dress-shopping experience. Here's an in-depth look at how AI is making a significant impact:

Personalized Recommendations: AI algorithms analyze a bride's preferences, body type, and wedding theme to suggest the most suitable dress styles. By leveraging machine learning, these systems refine their suggestions based on user feedback, ensuring increasingly tailored recommendations that match the bride's unique taste.

Virtual Try-Ons and Fittings: AI-powered virtual try-on technology allows brides to see how different dresses will look on their bodies without physically trying them on. This saves time and provides a comprehensive understanding of how a dress will fit and flow on the big day. Advanced AI can model fabric drape, movement, and lighting effects, providing a realistic preview.

AI-Enhanced Customization: Customization is vital in bridal fashion, and AI makes it more accessible and precise. AI tools enable brides to design their own dresses by selecting from various fabrics, cuts, and embellishments, visualizing the final product in real-time. These tools can also suggest adjustments to enhance fit and comfort based on the bride's measurements and posture.

Predictive Trend Analysis: AI analyzes vast amounts of data from fashion shows, social media, and historical trends to predict upcoming bridal fashion trends. This helps designers stay ahead of the curve and provides brides with insights into the latest styles and innovations.

Sustainable Fashion Solutions: With sustainability becoming a significant concern in fashion, AI plays a crucial role in promoting eco-friendly practices. AI can optimize material usage, reduce waste in the design and production process, and suggest sustainable alternatives for fabrics and decorations.

Enhanced Customer Service: AI-driven chatbots and virtual assistants provide instant customer support, answering queries about dress availability, customization options, and fitting appointments. These tools guide brides through the buying process, making it more convenient and efficient.

Data-Driven Insights for Retailers: For bridal fashion retailers, AI offers valuable insights into customer preferences and buying behaviors. This enables better inventory management, targeted marketing campaigns, and a more personalized shopping experience.

Let's examine how virtual try-ons have transformed bridal fashion through success stories.

Emma's Virtual Try-Ons Story

The impact of virtual try-ons in bridal fashion is best illustrated with Emma, a bride who was planning her wedding during the height of the COVID-19 pandemic. With lockdowns and social distancing measures in place, Emma turned to **Zoe by Jovani**, a virtual try-on service specifically for bridesmaid dresses and gowns. Using **Zoe**, she was able to have her bridesmaids upload their measurements and create digital avatars that closely resembled their physical appearances.

Emma and her bridesmaids spent hours exploring various dress designs, trying on different styles virtually from the comfort of their own homes. This tool allowed them to experiment with different colors, styles, and fits that complemented each bridesmaid's unique shape and preferences. The ability to see the dresses on their avatars helped the group make confident decisions without the need for in-person fittings. Finally, they settled on a beautiful set of gowns that perfectly matched the wedding's theme and aesthetic.

When the dresses arrived, they were a perfect match for each bridesmaid, both in fit and style. By offering a convenient, personalized, and interactive shopping experience, **Zoe by Jovani** helped Emma and her bridesmaids find the perfect dresses without the traditional stress and hassle of coordinating fittings across different locations. This innovative approach ensured that everyone looked and felt their best on the big day.

By offering a convenient, personalized, and interactive shopping experience, these tools are helping brides worldwide find their perfect dress without the traditional stress and hassle.

Moving forward, we'll examine how AI enhances dress recommendations for a personalized experience.

AI-Powered Dress Recommendations

AI-powered dress recommendations are transforming how brides discover their dream gowns, making the search more intuitive, efficient, and personalized. Traditional dress shopping can be overwhelming due to the countless styles, fabrics, and designs available. AI simplifies this process by offering suggestions that align with each bride's unique preferences and body type.

Alicia Hernandez-Whyle

AI algorithms analyze a bride's preferences, such as favorite colors, preferred styles, desired fit, and practical considerations like budget and wedding venue. These systems then suggest dresses that match these criteria, often presenting options brides might not have initially considered. The recommendations are continually refined through machine learning, which considers feedback from the bride as she interacts with the platform. This iterative process ensures that suggestions become increasingly tailored to her tastes.

For example, if a bride prefers vintage styles, the AI system might suggest dresses with lace details and classic silhouettes. Conversely, a bride seeking something modern might receive recommendations for minimalist gowns with clean lines and unique cuts. The AI's ability to cross-reference current trends, fashion data, and individual preferences results in a curated selection of dresses closely aligning with the bride's vision.

Integrating AI-powered recommendations and virtual try-ons creates a smooth and effortless shopping experience. Brides can explore recommended dresses in a virtual fitting room, try them on their digital avatar, and make informed decisions based on a realistic preview. Advanced AI technology can simulate fabric drape, movement, and lighting effects, providing a comprehensive understanding of how a dress will look and feel on the big day.

The real-time visualization capabilities of virtual try-ons are remarkable. Brides can rotate their digital selves to view the dress from every angle, ensuring the dress looks stunning from all perspectives. They can also experiment with different styles, fabrics, and colors, customizing the dress to match their personal preferences and wedding theme.

Moving forward, we'll examine how AI takes dress designs from concept to reality.

AI-Driven Design Creation: From Concept to Reality

AI technology empowers brides to actively participate in the design process, transforming their dream dresses into reality. Brides can prompt desired features and styles, using **Not Just a Label** and **CLO 3D** to create custom designs tailored to their vision.

These tools allow brides to input elements like neckline, sleeve length, silhouette, and decorative details. For instance, a bride may specify a mermaid silhouette with a sweetheart neckline, intricate lace patterns, and a long train. The AI generates designs incorporating these features, offering a range of options for refinement.

Alicia Hernandez-Whyle

AI analyzes vast amounts of design data, ensuring custom creations are unique yet feasible. Factors like fabric behavior and construction techniques are considered, making designs practical. Brides can experiment with combinations and variations, bringing their ideas to life quickly.

One bride, Chloe, used **Not Just a Label's** design tool to create her wedding dress. She envisioned a gown that combined elements of vintage elegance with modern sophistication. By inputting her preferences for antique lace and a contemporary A-line silhouette, the AI generated several designs that captured her vision. Chloe was able to tweak the details, such as adding pearl embellishments and adjusting the length of the train, until she arrived at her perfect dress. The final design was not only a reflection of her personal style but also a one-of-a-kind creation that made her wedding day even more special.

This AI-driven design approach democratizes the process of dress creation, giving brides the tools to be the designers of their own wedding attire. It bridges the gap between imagination and reality, allowing for a truly personalized and creative bridal fashion experience.

Next, let's explore AI in custom dress design.

Custom Dress Design With AI

Artificial intelligence is revolutionizing bridal fashion, particularly in custom dress design. AI empowers brides to collaborate closely with designers to create bespoke gowns that reflect their personal style. By streamlining the design process and enhancing communication, AI makes custom wedding dress creation more accessible and efficient.

AI captures detailed inputs from the bride, such as preferred silhouettes, neckline styles, and fabric types, to generate a comprehensive design brief. This ensures a clear understanding of the bride's vision from inception. By providing visual representations of potential designs, AI bridges the gap between abstract ideas and concrete designs. It facilitates ongoing communication by simulating changes in fabric or design and providing instant updated visuals, reducing the need for multiple fittings.

Additionally, AI translates the bride's descriptions into technical design language, preventing misunderstandings and ensuring both parties are aligned on design details. This dynamic feedback loop ensures the design evolves in line with the bride's preferences, making the custom dress design process more efficient and effective.

The collaboration between brides, designers, and AI continues with real-time simulations of the dress on a virtual model. Brides can see how different fabrics drape, how embellishments look in various lighting, and how the dress moves, all from home. This interactive process saves time and ensures the bride's vision is realized with precision.

Building on custom dress creation, let's explore AI's role in choosing and coordinating bridal accessories.

Accessorizing with AI

In bridal fashion, the perfect dress is just the beginning. The right accessories, whether jewelry, shoes, veils, or bouquets, are crucial for creating a memorable wedding look. AI technology is revolutionizing how brides select these complementary items, offering personalized recommendations that ensure a cohesive and stunning ensemble. Selecting the right accessories can be daunting with numerous options available.

AI-powered tools like **StyleMatch** simplify this process by analyzing the bride's dress and personal style to recommend accessories that harmonize perfectly. These tools consider the dress's style, color, fabric, and embellishments, along with the bride's preferences. For example, if the dress is a vintage-inspired lace gown, **StyleMatch** might suggest pearl jewelry and classic pumps. By gathering data on the bride's style and wedding theme, **StyleMatch** offers personalized accessory suggestions. The AI considers the overall vibe the bride wants to achieve, ensuring every accessory fits seamlessly into the larger picture.

Advanced AI tools offer virtual try-on capabilities, allowing brides to see how different accessories look with their dress in real time. Brides can experiment with various options and make informed decisions. **StyleMatch** provides insights into current bridal fashion trends and suggests popular accessories, helping brides stay fashionable and timeless. This comprehensive approach not only simplifies the process but also enhances the overall bridal fashion experience by ensuring that each accessory perfectly complements the bride's dress and personal style.

In addition to accessorizing, let's explore how AI helps in selecting attire for the entire bridal party.

Selecting Attire Beyond the Bride

Alicia Hernandez-Whyle

While the bride's dress is often the focal point of wedding fashion, the attire of the bridal party is also crucial in creating a cohesive and visually harmonious wedding ensemble. Coordinating attire for bridesmaids to complement the overall wedding theme can be challenging, especially with different body types, personal styles, and logistical constraints. AI technology, particularly through tools like **Zyler**, is making this process more manageable and efficient, ensuring the entire bridal party looks stunning and unified on the big day.

Zyler offers personalized suggestions that align with the wedding theme while accommodating the unique needs of each bridal party member. It analyzes the overall wedding theme, color palette, and the bride's dress to recommend complementary attire. For instance, for a romantic garden affair with a soft pastel palette, it might suggest bridesmaid dresses in shades of blush, lavender, or sage green, and coordinating ties or pocket squares for the groomsmen.

This results in a visually cohesive group that enhances the overall wedding ambiance. Additionally, **Zyler** uses virtual styling platforms where the bride can input her preferences, generating a selection of dresses with virtual try-on capabilities. It uses body scans or measurements to recommend perfectly fitting attire, eliminating the need for multiple fittings and ensuring everyone looks their best.

Beyond selection, **Zyler** simplifies group coordination. It suggests matching elements for groomsmen based on bridesmaid dresses, creating a harmonious look. Budget management features help brides find options within their budget, offering price comparisons and highlighting cost-effective choices without compromising style or quality.

Zyler also facilitates communication, allowing the bride to share attire options and gather feedback, streamlining decision-making, and ensuring everyone is aligned. This comprehensive approach simplifies the entire process, from selection to fitting and coordination, making the experience efficient and stress-free for the bride and her bridal party.

Our discussion continues with the role of AI in achieving a cohesive look for the groom and his groomsmen.

The Role of AI in Ensuring a Cohesive Wedding Ensemble

Choosing the right attire for the groom involves more than just picking a suit or tuxedo; it requires careful consideration of the wedding theme, color palette, and personal preferences. **The Knot** revolutionizes this process by providing tailored recommendations to ensure every detail is perfect. **The Knot** analyzes wedding details, such as the venue, theme, and color scheme, and the bride's dress to recommend suits or tuxedos that complement the overall look. For example, it might suggest classic black tuxedos for a formal evening wedding or casual linen suits in earth tones for a rustic outdoor wedding.

AI tools help select attire that matches or complements the wedding colors, suggesting specific shades for suits, shirts, ties, and pocket squares. **The Knot** also recommends suit and tuxedo styles that align with the wedding's formality and the groom's taste, from modern slim-fit suits to traditional three-piece ensembles. Additionally, **The Knot** uses body measurements for accurate fit and offers virtual fittings, ensuring a perfect look without multiple in-person fittings.

AI technology simplifies selecting and coordinating attire for the groom and groomsmen, ensuring their outfits complement the bride's dress and the wedding theme. It ensures consistency by aligning the groom and groomsmen's attire with the wedding theme and bridesmaids' dresses, creating a cohesive look. AI provides accurate fit recommendations and virtual fittings, saving time and reducing costs while offering budget-friendly options. It personalizes suggestions based on individual preferences and body types, ensuring comfort and confidence.

AI platforms facilitate idea sharing and collaborative decision-making among the bridal party, reducing stress and allowing everyone to focus on enjoying the celebration without last-minute wardrobe concerns.

Perfecting Wedding Hairstyles with BrideLook AI

When it comes to wedding hairstyles, both the bride and bridesmaids play crucial roles in creating a cohesive and enchanting look for the big day. The bride often opts for a signature hairstyle that reflects her personal style, while bridesmaids typically wear coordinated hairstyles that harmonize with the bride's look, often featuring soft braids, half-up and half-down styles, or sleek ponytails embellished with accessories.

BrideLook, an AI tool, is designed to assist brides and bridesmaids in visualizing and perfecting their wedding hairstyles. Using AI technology, **BrideLook** allows brides to upload their photos and explore a wide array of hairstyle options tailored to their face shape, dress style, and wedding theme.

Additionally, it provides bridesmaids the opportunity to collaborate and experiment with different styles, ensuring that everyone feels beautiful and confident on the special day. This AI-driven approach not only saves time during the planning process but also adds a fun and creative element to selecting the perfect bridal party hairstyles.

Let's delve into how AI assists in the preservation and care of wedding dresses.

Dress Preservation and Care

The wedding dress is a cherished memento from a bride's special day, representing a significant emotional and financial investment. Preserving this garment to maintain its pristine condition is essential. AI technology is revolutionizing dress preservation, offering personalized recommendations and professional services that ensure the dress remains beautiful.

AI tools identify the exact fabric composition of a wedding dress, ensuring precise care for each material. For delicate fabrics like silk and lace, AI provides different care guidelines compared to more robust materials like satin or taffeta. AI systems also identify stains and suggest appropriate treatment methods, ensuring marks from the wedding day are properly addressed. Additionally, these tools assess environmental conditions such as temperature, humidity, and light exposure, recommending optimal storage solutions to prevent damage.

AI platforms like **Zola** evaluate preservation services based on fabric specialization, customer reviews, and service quality. They compare costs and quality, helping brides find the best value within their budget.

In conclusion, as we step further into the digital age, artificial intelligence is poised to redefine bridal fashion, creating a seamless blend of tradition and innovation. AI technology brings numerous advantages to the industry, from personalized recommendations to virtual try-ons and AI-enhanced customization. These advancements not only streamline the dress-shopping process but also offer brides a more personalized, efficient, and enjoyable experience.

AI's impact on bridal fashion is profound, enabling brides to visualize and customize their wedding attire like never before. Through AI-powered recommendations, brides receive suggestions that align with their unique preferences, body types, and wedding themes, ensuring a perfect match. Virtual try-ons provide a realistic preview of how dresses will look and fit, saving time and reducing the stress of multiple fittings. Moreover, AI-

Alicia Hernandez-Whyle

driven design tools empower brides to be their own designers, transforming their dream dresses into reality with precision and creativity.

Chapter Nine

Invitations and Guest Management with AI

Planning a wedding involves countless details, but one of the most significant tasks is managing invitations and guest lists. Traditionally, this process has been time-consuming and prone to human error, leading to added stress for couples. However, the advent of artificial intelligence (AI) has revolutionized wedding planning, particularly in the realm of guest management. This chapter delves into the transformative power of AI in streamlining these processes, making them more efficient, personalized, and eco-friendly. From creating your guest list to managing RSVPs, and from designing invitations to ensuring sustainability, AI can be a game-changer, providing tools that save time, enhance communication, and deliver a seamless experience for both the couple and their guests.

As we continue to delve deeper into the wedding planning process, one of the first and most crucial steps is creating your guest list, a task that sets the foundation for many other decisions to follow.

Creating a Guest List

Creating a guest list is one of the most significant tasks in wedding planning, setting the tone for your entire event. Start by listing immediate family members from both sides, including parents, siblings, grandparents, and close relatives. Add your closest friends who you can't imagine celebrating without. Organize your list into categories such as family, friends, coworkers, and acquaintances. This will help you see where you can make adjustments if necessary. It's also helpful to create an A-list of must-have guests and a B-list of people you'd like to invite if your budget and venue allow.

Discuss your list with your partner, parents, and other contributors to your wedding budget. They might have additional names or concerns to address. Ensure your guest list aligns with your venue's capacity and your budget to avoid over-inviting and creating a situation where you need to make last-minute cuts. Be flexible and prepared for changes, as some guests may not be able to attend, and you may need to make adjustments accordingly.

Now that you have a comprehensive guest list, let's explore how AI can simplify and enhance your guest management process, ensuring everything runs smoothly and efficiently.

How AI can Aid with Guest Management

AI tools integrate data from various sources to ensure no important person is left out and categorize guests into various groups, making it easier to plan seating arrangements and other logistics later on.

For instance, **Zola's** guest list manager allows you to import contacts from social media accounts and email lists, deduplicating entries, identifying relationships, and suggesting additional guests based on your social networks. This ensures that your guest list is comprehensive and organized, saving you countless hours of manual entry and sorting.

Additionally, **The Knot** offers a similar guest list management tool that integrates seamlessly with other wedding planning features. It categorizes guests, tracks RSVPs, and helps with seating chart creation, ensuring every aspect of guest management is streamlined.

Furthermore, **Microsoft Outlook** can be integrated with other wedding planning apps to provide a seamless flow of information, ensuring that updates are synchronized across all your planning tools. This can be particularly useful for couples who have a large number of guests and need to ensure accuracy and completeness in their guest list.

Using these AI-powered tools ensures accuracy, saves time, and reduces the stress associated with manual guest list creation. They provide a centralized platform for managing guest information, making it easier to keep track of who is invited, who has responded, and any specific requirements they might have.

Having leveraged AI to streamline your guest management process, the next crucial step is to ensure your guests are informed and prepared by sending out save-the-dates and formal invitations.

Sending Save-the-Dates and Invitations

Once the guest list is in place, the next step is to send out save-the-dates and invitations. AI can play a crucial role here by offering digital solutions that not only save time but also add a touch of sophistication to your wedding communications. Digital invitations can be designed with AI-powered platforms that provide customizable templates, ensuring that your invites reflect your wedding theme and personal style.

Canva's AI-powered design assistant can help you create stunning invitations by offering design suggestions, layout options, and color palettes that match your wedding theme. Furthermore, platforms like **Minted** use AI to match your invitation design with complementary stationery items, such as thank-you cards and wedding programs, ensuring a cohesive aesthetic throughout your wedding communications.

Additionally, **Paperless Post** integrates AI to track open rates, RSVPs, and guest interactions, giving you real-time insights into your invitation campaign's effectiveness. This helps ensure that no invitation gets lost or overlooked and allows you to follow up with guests who may not have responded.

These tools provide a hassle-free way to design and send invitations, ensuring that they are visually appealing and consistent with your wedding theme. They also offer tracking and management features that help you stay on top of RSVPs and guest interactions, making the process more efficient and less stressful.

Once your save-the-dates and invitations are sent, the next essential task is managing RSVPs to keep track of who will be attending your special day.

Managing RSVPs and Guest Lists with Smart Tools

Efficiently managing RSVPs is essential for ensuring a well-organized wedding. Start by setting a clear RSVP deadline, typically three to four weeks before the wedding date, to finalize numbers for catering and seating. Provide multiple RSVP options, such as mail-in cards, email, phone, or a wedding website form, to cater to different preferences.

Track responses diligently using a spreadsheet, wedding planning software, or an AI-powered tool, noting who has responded, their meal choices, and any special requests. A week before the deadline, follow up with non-responders through gentle reminder emails, phone calls, or text messages. Compile all responses into a master guest list, including contact information and relevant notes.

Finally, communicate the final guest count to your venue, caterer, and other vendors, ensuring they have all the necessary information to accommodate your guests.

Leveraging AI to Simplify Guest Management

AI-driven RSVP management systems track responses in real time, send reminders to those who haven't replied, and update guest lists automatically. These systems can also identify potential issues, such as overbooking or underbooking, and suggest solutions.

WeddingWire's guest list manager provides automated updates and communication tools to keep guests informed. It integrates with other wedding planning features, making it easy to manage all aspects of your wedding from a single platform.

RSVPify's intelligent RSVP tracking features allow you to manage responses from multiple events, send automated reminders, and track guest preferences all in one place. This ensures that your catering is tailored to your guests' needs, reducing food waste and enhancing the dining experience.

Similarly, **Joy's** platform provides a holistic view of your guest list, integrating RSVPs with your wedding website and offering features like meal selection tracking and accommodation planning. This helps you stay organized and ensures that all guest information is easily accessible.

Moreover, **AllSeated's** AI-powered seating chart tool allows you to visualize your venue and arrange seating with ease. It also provides real-time updates on RSVPs, making it easier to manage last-minute changes and ensure that everyone is accounted for.

These tools streamline the RSVP process, reduce the likelihood of errors, and provide real-time insights into guest responses. This allows you to plan more effectively and ensure that all guest needs are met, resulting in a smoother and more enjoyable wedding experience.

With RSVPs being managed, let's explore how AI can help you design and create beautiful digital and traditional invitations that capture the essence of your wedding.

Creating Digital and Traditional Invitations Using AI

When it comes to designing invitations, whether digital or traditional, AI offers a range of tools that make the process both creative and efficient. AI-powered design platforms provide a plethora of templates, fonts, and color schemes, allowing you to craft beautiful and unique invitations.

Adobe Spark's AI-driven design assistant helps you create professional-quality invitations by suggesting design elements that enhance your theme. It offers a wide range of templates and customization options, allowing you to create unique and personalized invitations.

Evite's platform offers both digital and print options, allowing you to manage your invitations seamlessly across different formats. It also provides eco-friendly recommendations, such as recycled paper options and carbon offset services, ensuring that your wedding communications are sustainable.

Additionally, **Bliss & Bone** offers interactive digital invitations that include elements such as videos, music, and animated graphics. These invitations provide a unique and memorable experience for your guests, setting the tone for your wedding from the moment they receive their invite.

Using AI-powered design tools allows you to create stunning invitations that reflect your personal style and wedding theme. These tools also offer eco-friendly options and interactive features that enhance the guest experience and ensure that your invitations are both beautiful and sustainable.

Now that your invitations are beautifully crafted, it's time to focus on personalizing guest experiences to make your wedding truly unforgettable.

Personalizing Guest Experiences

One of the most significant advantages of using AI in guest management is the ability to personalize the guest experience. AI can analyze data to offer tailored recommendations, such as personalized welcome messages, customized seating arrangements, and individualized favors.

WedPics allows guests to upload and share photos in real time, creating a collaborative wedding album that captures every moment. It also offers personalized event schedules, interactive maps, and custom messages, ensuring that each guest feels special and connected to your wedding journey.

Wedivite's personalized wedding app offers guests a tailored experience, with features like event schedules, interactive maps, and custom messages. It also integrates with social media, allowing guests to share their experiences and stay connected.

Minted's AI-powered platform offers personalized wedding favors, such as custom messages or unique gifts that reflect each guest's preferences and interests. This ensures that each guest receives a memorable and meaningful token of appreciation.

While personalizing your guests' experiences, it's also important to consider eco-friendly options that can make your wedding both memorable and environmentally conscious.

Eco-Friendly Options

In today's world, sustainability is a vital factor for many couples planning their weddings. AI can assist in finding and implementing eco-friendly solutions for both invitations and guest management.

Eco-friendly platforms like **Greenvelope** AI to offer sustainable wedding solutions. **Greenvelope** provides digital invitation services with a focus on sustainability, offering carbon offset options and eco-friendly designs.

Glo's platform integrates AI to help you find and connect with eco-conscious vendors, ensuring that every aspect of your wedding is aligned with your environmental values. Additionally, **Evite** provides recommendations for recycled paper options and carbon offset services, ensuring that your wedding communications are sustainable.

Using these AI-powered tools ensures that your wedding planning process is environmentally responsible. They offer eco-friendly options for invitations and guest management, helping you minimize your carbon footprint and make ethical choices throughout your planning process.

To see eco-friendly wedding practices in action, let's look at a case study of Sarah and Tom's beautifully sustainable wedding.

Case Study: Jessica and Tom's Eco-Friendly Wedding

To better understand the impact of AI on wedding planning, consider the story of Jessica and Tom, a tech-savvy couple from California who wanted their wedding to reflect their deep commitment to sustainability. This commitment was deeply personal, rooted in a life experience that profoundly shaped their values.

Several years before their engagement, Jessica and Tom experienced a devastating wildfire that swept through their hometown in California. The fire, driven by drought, destroyed homes, wildlife habitats, and thousands of acres of forest. Jessica's childhood home was among those lost, and the couple spent weeks helping their community recover. The emotional toll of witnessing the destruction of their environment made them acutely aware of the urgent need for environmental stewardship.

When it came time to plan their wedding, Jessica and Tom knew they wanted to minimize their environmental impact. They turned to AI-powered tools to achieve this goal.

They started by using **Zola** to compile their guest list. The AI-powered tool allowed them to seamlessly import contacts from their social media accounts and email lists, ensuring that no one was left out. This streamlined process not only saved time but also reduced the likelihood of paper invitations, aligning with their commitment to sustainability.

For their invitations, Jessica and Tom chose **Greenvelope**, an AI-driven platform that specializes in digital save-the-dates and invitations. They selected eco-friendly templates that perfectly matched their wedding theme, significantly reducing paper waste.

Their use of AI tools for managing the guest list and invitations not only reflected their commitment to sustainability but also made the entire process smoother and more environmentally friendly. By embracing technology, Jessica and Tom were able to create a wedding that honored their values, proving that it is possible to celebrate love while also caring for the planet.

Alicia Hernandez-Whyle

By employing AI's capabilities, you can create a guest list with ease, send out beautiful and timely invitations, manage RSVPs efficiently, and personalize the guest experience, all while maintaining a commitment to sustainability.

With your invitations dispatched and guests eagerly anticipating the event, it's time to focus on the intricate details of coordinating the ceremony to ensure everything unfolds perfectly.

Part Four: The Big Day

Alicia Hernandez-Whyle

Chapter Ten

Ceremony Coordination

Planning the ceremony is a key element in preparing for your wedding day. Coordinating numerous aspects is essential to creating a ceremony that is heartfelt, customized, and flawlessly executed. The ceremony is the heart of the wedding day, where the couple publicly declares their love and commitment. A well-planned ceremony sets the tone for the entire event and creates lasting memories for the couple and their guests. This chapter will guide you through the essential elements of ceremony planning, providing practical tips and insights to help you create a beautiful and seamless ceremony.

Let's now explore how AI technology can assist in planning a seamless and personalized wedding ceremony.

Utilizing AI Technology for Ceremony Planning

AI technology can significantly enhance the planning and execution of the wedding ceremony. AI-powered tools like **Joy** or **WeddingHappy** can help manage timelines, send reminders, and track tasks to ensure that nothing is overlooked. AI can also assist in crafting personalized vows or selecting readings by suggesting content based on the couple's preferences and relationship history.

Virtual reality tools like **The Venue Report** also offer a virtual walkthrough of the ceremony, allowing the couple and wedding party to visualize the setup and practice their roles in a simulated environment.

Let's now delve into the detailed steps involved in creating a seamless and memorable wedding ceremony.

Planning the Ceremony Details

Selecting the officiant is one of the most significant decisions in wedding planning, as this individual plays a pivotal role in guiding the couple through their vows and making the union official. The officiant sets the tone for the ceremony, so it's essential to find someone who resonates with the couple's vision and values. Several factors should be considered when choosing an officiant, including their availability, willingness to travel, and their style and approach to conducting the ceremony. Some officiants may have a more traditional and formal style, while others might offer a more relaxed and personalized approach.

Meeting with potential officiants beforehand is crucial to ensure a good fit. This allows the couple to discuss their expectations, ceremony preferences, and any specific traditions or customs they wish to incorporate. It also provides an opportunity to gauge the officiant's personality and see how well they connect with the couple.

AI can be a powerful tool in assisting couples with this important decision. Platforms like **Joy** and **WedSites** offer AI-powered features that streamline the process of finding and selecting the perfect officiant. **Joy's** AI-driven matching algorithms, for example, can connect couples with officiants who align with their preferences. By inputting specific criteria such as the desired ceremony style, religious or spiritual considerations, and even personality traits, couples receive a compile list of officiants who best meet their needs, saving time and ensuring the options presented align with their vision.

HoneyBook can track officiants' availability in real-time, automatically suggesting those who are available on the couple's wedding date and within the required location, reducing back-and-forth communication and minimizing the risk of any last-minute conflicts.

Furthermore, AI platforms like **WedSites** allow for virtual meetings between couples and potential officiants, which is particularly useful for those who may not be able to meet in person due to geographical distances. These platforms also analyze reviews and feedback from other couples, providing valuable insights into the officiant's strengths and weaknesses, helping the couple make an informed decision.

As we continue planning, it's important to address inclusivity and sensitivity to ensure that your ceremony is welcoming and respectful to all guests.

Inclusivity and Sensitivity

Creating an inclusive ceremony ensures that all guests feel welcome and valued. This involves considering the needs of guests with disabilities by providing wheelchair-accessible seating and pathways, offering sign language interpreters, or having printed materials in Braille. Sensory sensitivities can be accommodated by providing quiet areas or earplugs for guests who may be overwhelmed by loud music or crowded spaces. Additionally, being sensitive to the cultural and religious backgrounds of all guests can make the ceremony more inclusive.

This could involve incorporating elements from different traditions or ensuring that rituals are explained for those who may be unfamiliar with them, enriching the ceremony by highlighting the diversity of the couple's community. **Joy** can help manage and communicate these details effectively to ensure inclusivity and sensitivity.

As we continue our planning, selecting the right music for your ceremony is essential to set the tone and evoke the desired emotions with the right music.

Selecting Ceremony Music

Music is crucial in establishing the ceremony's atmosphere and enhancing its emotional highlights. Selecting the right ceremony music involves choosing pieces for key segments such as the processional, the signing of the register, and the recessional. The processional music should be elegant and reflective of the couple's style, while the music during the signing of the register often provides a serene backdrop. The recessional music, which plays as the newlyweds exit, is usually more celebratory and upbeat. Couples can opt for live musicians, such as string quartets or soloists, or pre-recorded tracks to set the mood. Coordinating with musicians or sound technicians is essential to ensure smooth transitions and that the music aligns perfectly with the planned timing of events.

AI can play a significant role in helping couples select and coordinate their ceremony music. For instance, AI-powered platforms like **Spotify** and **Pandora** can analyze the couple's music preferences and suggest song choices that match their desired vibe for each segment of the ceremony. These platforms can also create custom playlists that can be easily shared with musicians or sound technicians, ensuring everyone is on the same page. Additionally, AI tools like **Soundtrack Your Brand** can help in curating a personalized music experience, adjusting the playlist dynamically based on the ceremony's flow.

When choosing ceremony music, couples should consider not only their personal preferences but also the venue's acoustics and the overall theme of the wedding. For outdoor ceremonies, it's important to choose music that carries well in open spaces, while indoor venues may require a different approach to sound balance. Couples should also plan a few moments to discuss their selections with the officiant to ensure that the music complements the key moments of the ceremony.

Having addressed the ceremony music, let's now focus on décor and venue setup, essential for creating a visually stunning and cohesive environment.

Decor and Venue Setup

When planning your wedding, the venue and décor are not merely physical settings; they are the stage where your love story will unfold. It's not just about arranging furniture and decorations; it's about crafting an experience that resonates emotionally with everyone present, creating memories that will last a lifetime.

Start by envisioning how you want your guests to feel as they step into the space. The layout should be carefully considered, ensuring that the seating arrangement invites connection and intimacy, with loved ones positioned to clearly see your exchange of vows. Whether your ceremony is indoors or outdoors, comfort is key. For outdoor venues, think about the comfort of your guests offering cozy blankets for a chill in the air or providing shade from the sun so they can fully immerse themselves in the beauty of the day without distraction.

The season in which your wedding takes place can also influence your décor choices, adding a special touch that reflects the time of year. For instance, a winter wedding might feature rich, warm tones and cozy textures, creating a sense of warmth and intimacy, while a spring wedding could incorporate fresh, pastel colors and delicate floral arrangements, evoking a sense of renewal and new beginnings. By aligning your décor with the season, you can create a cohesive and immersive environment that enhances the overall ambiance of your ceremony.

Practicality is just as important as style. Ensure that seating arrangements are not only visually appealing but also comfortable and accessible for all guests. Consider the needs of elderly guests or those with mobility issues, and make sure that walkways and seating areas are easily navigable. The flow of the space should allow guests to move gracefully from one emotional moment to the next, from the anticipation of your entrance to the joy of your exit as newlyweds.

To manage and track all these details, tools like **WedPlanner Pro** can be invaluable, ensuring that every aspect of the décor is accounted for and executed as planned. Meanwhile, **AllSeated** or **Roomstyler** can create 3D renderings of the venue with the chosen décor, allowing you to see how everything will look before the big day and make adjustments as needed. These tools provide peace of mind, knowing that your vision will be brought to life exactly as you imagined.

Before the big day, take a quiet moment with your planner or venue coordinator to walk through the space. Imagine how it will all come together, how it will look; feel and, most importantly, how it will touch the hearts of everyone who shares this special day with you. This walk-through is not just a final check, but a moment to fully embrace the journey you've taken in planning this day, ensuring that every detail reflects the love and care you've put into making your wedding truly unforgettable.

With the décor and venue setup meticulously planned, it's time to shift focus to guest coordination, ensuring that every attendee experiences the same seamless and heartfelt atmosphere you've worked so hard to create.

Guest Coordination

Effective guest coordination is crucial to creating a smooth and enjoyable experience for everyone involved. From the moment guests arrive, clear signage and friendly ushers can guide them to their seats and help them navigate the venue with ease. Providing a detailed program or schedule of the ceremony is also key, allowing guests to know what to expect and when, ensuring they feel informed and engaged throughout the event. Having a designated point person or coordinator available to address any questions or concerns on the day of the wedding can greatly enhance guest comfort and reduce any potential stress.

Managing the flow of guests before, during, and after the ceremony is vital to preventing congestion and confusion. Thoughtful planning ensures a relaxed and enjoyable atmosphere for both the couple and their guests. Tools like RSVPify can streamline this process by helping to manage guest lists, seating arrangements, and communication, ensuring everything runs smoothly on the day.

Once guest coordination is in place, the next step is rehearsing the ceremony. This rehearsal is essential for ensuring a seamless and confident execution, giving everyone involved a clear understanding of their roles and what to expect during the big day.

Rehearsing the Ceremony

Rehearsing the ceremony is a vital step to ensure that everyone involved knows their roles and the sequence of events. A rehearsal typically takes place a day or two before the wedding and includes the wedding party, the officiant, and any musicians or readers. During the rehearsal, the coordinator or planner walks everyone through the ceremony step-by-step, from the processional to the recessional. This rehearsal is an opportunity to finalize details such as the timing of entrances, the order of events, and the positioning of the wedding party. It allows the couple and their attendants to practice their movements, ensuring they are comfortable and confident on the big day.

AI-powered virtual reality (VR) tools offers a virtual walkthrough of the ceremony, allowing the couple and wedding party to visualize the setup and practice their roles in a simulated environment.

As we wrap up the rehearsal details, let's turn our attention to photography and videography coordination.

Photography and Videography Coordination

Your wedding day is filled with moments that you'll want to remember forever, making the coordination with photographers and videographers essential. These professionals are responsible for capturing the magic of your ceremony and preserving the memories in a way that reflects the beauty and emotion of the day. To ensure they can do their best work without disrupting the flow of the ceremony, it's crucial to have a well thought-out plan in place.

Start by discussing the ceremony flow and key moments with your photography and videography team well in advance. This conversation helps them understand the timeline and pinpoint the most important parts of the ceremony that need to be captured.

For example, moments like the exchange of vows, the first kiss, and the couple's entrance and exit are often the highlights, and ensuring these are captured from the best angles is essential. Sharing the ceremony timeline allows the media team to prepare for these moments, ensuring they're in the right place at the right time.

Another important aspect of coordination is planning the placement and movement of the photographers and videographers during the ceremony. The goal is to capture stunning visuals without interfering with the proceedings.

Discussing this with your media team can help them find unobtrusive positions where they can operate effectively without drawing attention away from the ceremony. This careful planning helps maintain the solemnity and flow of the event while still allowing for beautiful photography and videography.

Clear communication is key to a successful partnership with your media team. Creating a shot list of must-have moments can be incredibly helpful, ensuring that the photographers and videographers focus on the aspects of the ceremony that are most important to you. Whether it's a close-up of your exchange of rings or a wide shot of your entire wedding party, a shot list keeps everyone aligned with your vision. Tools like **Trello** can be invaluable for managing and communicating these details, allowing you to share the shot list, timeline, and other important notes with your media team in an organized way.

With the photography and videography arrangements thoughtfully coordinated, you can rest assured that every special moment will be captured beautifully.

As the ceremony draws to a close and the key moments are captured, the next crucial aspect to consider is the coordination of post-ceremony logistics. Ensuring a smooth transition from the ceremony to the reception is essential for maintaining the day's flow and keeping the celebration moving seamlessly.

Post-Ceremony Logistics

As the ceremony concludes, the focus shifts to managing several important logistics that ensure the celebration continues smoothly. One of the first steps is the signing of the marriage license, a crucial task that legally binds the union. This moment, while often overlooked in the excitement of the day, is essential and should be coordinated carefully to avoid any delays or disruptions. Ensuring that the officiant, witnesses, and the couple are all aware of when and where this will take place can streamline the process, allowing everyone to move on to the festivities without unnecessary waiting.

Following the signing, many couples choose to organize a receiving line or a designated greeting area where they can personally interact with their guests and receive congratulations. This tradition offers a special opportunity to thank each guest for attending and share a brief moment with them, creating personal connections that enhance the warmth and joy of the day. Planning this part of the day carefully; with consideration for the venue's layout and the number of guests can help maintain the flow of the event, preventing bottlenecks or long waits.

Transitioning guests from the ceremony to the reception is another critical element of post-ceremony logistics. This transition should be as seamless as possible, with clear instructions and guidance provided to guests. Whether through signage, ushers, or announcements, it's important to ensure that guests know where to go next and how to get there. For ceremonies and receptions held at different locations, coordinating transportation or providing clear driving directions can help avoid confusion and keep the day running smoothly.

Additionally, it's essential to plan for the collection and safe transport of any personal or decorative items from the ceremony venue to the reception. This might include floral arrangements, ceremonial items, or even gifts that were presented during the ceremony. Assigning a trusted person or team to handle this task ensures that nothing is left behind.

Using tools like **Joy** can significantly ease the management of these post-ceremony logistics. Joy offers features that help track every detail, ensuring that tasks are completed as planned and that the transition from the ceremony to the reception is smooth and enjoyable for both the couple and their guests.

With post-ceremony logistics carefully coordinated, the couple can move effortlessly into the next phase of their celebration, confident that every detail has been handled with care. This thoughtful planning allows the focus to remain on what truly matters celebrating the love and commitment that the day represents.

Personalizing Your Ceremony Script

A well-crafted ceremony script is the backbone of a memorable wedding ceremony, outlining every word and action from start to finish. Typically, the script includes the officiant's welcome message, readings, vows, the exchange of rings, and any special rituals or unity ceremonies the couple wishes to incorporate. A good script balances tradition and personalization, reflecting the couple's unique love story while maintaining a coherent structure.

Reviewing and rehearsing the script with the official and participants ensures smooth delivery and timing on the big day. Including meaningful anecdotes, favorite quotes, or even humor can make the ceremony more engaging and heartfelt for both the couple and their guests.

Providing sample ceremony scripts can help couples visualize and plan their own ceremony. For example, a traditional religious script might include specific prayers, hymns, and readings relevant to the couple's faith. A non-religious script could focus on personal vows, meaningful readings, and symbolic actions, while an interfaith script can blend elements from different religious traditions to honor both faiths. These examples can serve as a starting point, allowing couples to customize and adapt them to fit their unique preferences and needs.

ChatGPT can generate customized ceremony scripts based on the couple's preferences, ensuring a personalized and meaningful ceremony.

Let's now look into the importance of having a backup plan for your ceremony.

Backup Plans

Having backup plans, especially for outdoor ceremonies, is not just a precaution; it is a necessity for ensuring that your wedding day remains beautiful and memorable, no matter what challenges arise. Outdoor weddings offer a unique and picturesque setting, but they also come with unpredictable variables, such as weather. It is essential to have contingency plans in place to address these potential disruptions.

One of the most critical backup strategies is arranging for tents or securing an indoor venue as an alternative in case of adverse weather conditions. Whether it is a sudden shower of rain, high winds, or unseasonable temperatures, having a sheltered option ensures that the ceremony can proceed smoothly without compromising the comfort of your guests or the integrity of your event. Flexibility is key here; being open to adjusting timelines or even slightly altering the day's schedule can help accommodate last-minute changes without causing undue stress.

In addition to weather-related contingencies, it is wise to have backup plans for other aspects of the ceremony. This could include alternative arrangements for musicians if they are unable to perform due to unforeseen circumstances or adjustments in seating arrangements if the original setup becomes unworkable. Having these contingency plans in place not only protects the overall flow of the day but also helps maintain the atmosphere and experience you have meticulously planned.

Communication is another crucial element of effective contingency planning. It is important that all parties involved, such as planners, vendors, and even guests, are aware of the backup plans and know what to expect if they need to be implemented. This level of preparedness ensures that everyone is on the same page, allowing the day to proceed with as little disruption as possible.

To help manage these backup plans, tools like **WeddingHappy** can be incredibly useful. **WeddingHappy** allows you to create and organize contingency plans, making sure all options are considered and communicated effectively. This app can track your plans, send reminders, and ensure that nothing falls through the cracks, giving you peace of mind as you approach your big day.

With robust backup plans in place, you can approach your wedding day with confidence, knowing that you are prepared for any situation that might arise. Now, let's turn our attention to emergency preparedness, ensuring that you are ready to handle any unexpected emergencies that may occur on your wedding day.

Legal Considerations

Legal requirements for the ceremony include obtaining a marriage license, ensuring the officiant is legally recognized to perform the ceremony, and completing any necessary paperwork. Understanding and fulfilling these legal aspects are crucial for the marriage to be recognized officially. It is important to research the specific legal requirements in the couple's jurisdiction and ensure all documents are prepared and submitted in a timely manner.

Additionally, confirming the officiant's credentials and any necessary permits for the venue can prevent last-minute legal issues. By addressing these legal considerations well in advance, the couple can ensure a smooth and legally binding ceremony. **Joy** can help track and manage these legal requirements, ensuring that all necessary steps are completed on time.

In conclusion, thorough planning and attention to detail are essential for a successful wedding ceremony. By considering all aspects, from selecting the officiant and crafting personalized vows to ensuring inclusivity and managing guest coordination, couples can create a meaningful and memorable event. Leveraging AI technology, coordinating with photographers and videographers, and having backup plans in place can further enhance the planning process.

Chapter Eleven

Wedding Day Logistics: Staying on Track

The wedding day is the culmination of months, sometimes years, of meticulous planning and anticipation. Every detail, from the ceremony to the reception, needs to be perfectly coordinated to ensure a seamless and memorable experience. A well-orchestrated event can mean the difference between a chaotic day and a smooth, joyous celebration. Each element, from the timing of the bridal party's entrance to the delivery of the cake, must be synchronized to create a harmonious flow.

In recent years, technology, particularly artificial intelligence (AI), has become increasingly significant in wedding planning. AI tools are revolutionizing how couples and planners approach logistics, offering innovative solutions to traditional challenges. These tools can automate schedules, provide personalized recommendations, and solve problems in real-time, enhancing the efficiency and effectiveness of wedding day management. By predicting potential issues and providing contingency plans, AI ensures that nothing is left to chance. Utilizing these technologies allows couples to enjoy a stress-free wedding day, confident that every aspect is handled with precision and care.

AI also assists in communication and coordination among vendors, ensuring everyone involved is on the same page. This reduces misunderstandings and last-minute changes, contributing to a smooth execution of the day's events. Combining meticulous planning with cutting-edge technology ensures that the wedding day unfolds flawlessly, creating lasting memories for the couple and their guests.

Creating a Day-of-Timeline

A well-crafted day-of timeline is the backbone of any successful wedding day, ensuring that each moment flows seamlessly into the next. This detailed schedule helps keep everyone on track, from the wedding party to the vendors, reducing stress and preventing last-minute chaos.

Here's a step-by-step guide to crafting a comprehensive timeline, along with insights into how AI tools can enhance this process through dynamic schedule creation and adjustment.

Step-by-Step Guide to Crafting a Detailed Timeline

Step 1: Start with the Ceremony Time

The first step in crafting a detailed wedding timeline is to determine the ceremony start time, which serves as the anchor for the entire day's schedule. Whether you choose a morning, afternoon, or evening ceremony, this decision will influence the timing of all other events throughout the day. Once the ceremony time is set, you can begin working backward to plan all pre-ceremony activities, such as hair, makeup, and photography sessions, ensuring that everything aligns smoothly with the start of the ceremony.

Step 2: List All the Major Events of the Day

With the ceremony time established, the next step is to list all the major events that will take place on your wedding day. This includes key moments like hair and makeup, getting dressed, the first look, the ceremony itself, cocktail hour, dinner, speeches, dancing, and the grand exit. Don't forget to account for any religious or cultural rituals that may need to be included, as well as any special traditions that are important to you. By identifying all these events, you can create a comprehensive outline of your day.

Step 3: Allocate Time Blocks for Each Event

After listing the major events, it is important to allocate specific time blocks for each one. For instance, you might plan for 60-90 minutes for the bride's hair and makeup and 30-45 minutes for each bridesmaid. Getting dressed should be allocated at least 30 minutes, particularly for the bride, who may need assistance with her gown. The first look and pre-ceremony photos typically require 1-2 hours, depending on the locations and the number of photos desired. The ceremony itself may take 20-45 minutes, followed by a 1-hour cocktail hour. Finally, include time for reception activities like dinner, speeches, and dancing, ensuring that each event has ample time to unfold naturally.

Step 4: Incorporate Buffer Time

Incorporating buffer time into your timeline is crucial for keeping the day on track. Adding extra time between events allows for unexpected delays, which are often inevitable on such a busy day. For example, you might include 15-30 minutes between the end of hair and makeup and the start of getting dressed to account for any last-minute adjustments. If your ceremony and reception are at different locations, be sure to account for travel time and potential traffic. Buffer time helps to ensure that small hiccups don't disrupt the overall flow of the day.

Step 5: Coordinate with Vendors

Coordinating with vendors is a key part of creating a successful wedding timeline. It is essential to communicate your timeline with all vendors involved, including the photographer, videographer, florist, and caterer, to ensure they have enough time to set up and perform their tasks efficiently. Be open to adjustments based on vendor input, as they may have specific needs or valuable suggestions that could enhance the timeline. This coordination helps to ensure that every aspect of the day runs smoothly and according to plan.

Step 6: Create a Detailed Timeline

Once the major events and vendor coordination are in place, it is time to create a detailed timeline. Using a spreadsheet or a wedding planning tool like **Google Sheets**, **Aisle Planner**, or **WeddingHappy**, you can organize each event by specific times, noting who is involved and where it will take place. Make sure to include the arrival times for all vendors and any other critical milestones. This detailed timeline serves as a blueprint for the day, helping everyone involved to stay on schedule.

Step 7: Share the Timeline

With your detailed timeline ready, the next step is to share it with all key participants. Ensure that your bridal party, family members, officiant, and vendors receive the timeline well in advance and that they understand their roles and timing. This communication is crucial for avoiding confusion and ensuring that everyone is on the same page. It is also a good idea to print copies of the timeline for your planner, coordinator, and anyone else who might need one on the day of the wedding.

Step 8: Be Flexible and Prepared for Adjustments

Even the most meticulously planned timelines may require adjustments on the day of the wedding. It is important to remain flexible and prepared to make changes as needed. Whether it is accommodating a delay or adjusting the schedule due to unforeseen circumstances, being open to modifications can help keep the day stress-free. Additionally, having a backup plan for key events, such as an indoor option for an outdoor ceremony, ensures that you are prepared for any eventuality.

Step 9: Finalize the Timeline

In the final step, review the timeline with your wedding planner or coordinator to ensure everything is set and ready to go. This is also the time to confirm all details with your vendors, ideally a week before the wedding, to make sure everyone is aligned and aware of their responsibilities. Finalizing the timeline gives you peace of mind, knowing that everything is organized and ready for your big day.

Step 10: Enjoy Your Day

On your wedding day, trust in the timeline you've created and focus on enjoying every moment. With careful planning and preparation, you can relax and savor the experience, knowing that all the details have been taken care of and that your day will unfold beautifully.

By following these steps and leveraging the power of AI, you can create a detailed, adaptable, and stress-free timeline that ensures your wedding day unfolds flawlessly.

Now, let's explore how modern technology, particularly AI tools, enhances this process by offering dynamic schedule creation and adjustment capabilities.

AI for Dynamic Schedule Creation

Incorporating AI tools into the creation and management of your wedding day timeline can significantly enhance its efficiency and adaptability. Here's how:

Automated Schedule Creation: AI-powered wedding planning platforms can automatically generate a detailed timeline based on your wedding details and preferences. By inputting basic information, such as the ceremony and reception start times, the tool can suggest a comprehensive schedule, complete with recommended time allocations for each activity. **Riley & Grey** offers luxury wedding planning features, including an automated timeline tool that helps couples organize their day by suggesting time allocations and schedules based on their preferences.

Personalized Recommendations: These tools analyze data from thousands of weddings to provide personalized suggestions tailored to your specific needs. Whether it's the ideal length of a cocktail hour or the best time to cut the cake, AI can offer insights that help optimize your timeline.

Real-time Updates and Ajustments: One of the most significant advantages of AI is its ability to make real-time adjustments. If a delay occurs, such as the photographer running late or unexpected weather changes, AI tools can dynamically update the schedule, notifying all relevant parties instantly. This ensures that the day remains on track despite any unforeseen changes. Tools like **The Knot, Zola,** and **WhatsApp** facilitate these updates, ensuring a seamless, well-coordinated event that adapts effortlessly to any last-minute changes.

Coordination and Communication: AI tools can also streamline communication between the couple, wedding planner, and vendors. By integrating with various communication platforms, these tools ensure everyone is updated about any changes or adjustments, reducing the risk of miscommunication.

Stress Reduction: Ultimately, utilizing AI for dynamic schedule creation and adjustment reduces the stress associated with wedding day logistics. Couples can enjoy their special day, knowing that the timeline is being managed efficiently and any issues will be promptly addressed.

Let's not see how AI driven tools can aid with transport coordination.

Alicia Hernandez-Whyle

Coordinating Transportation

Coordinating transportation for a wedding can be complex, especially considering the varied needs of the wedding party and guests. Proper planning ensures timely arrivals at the ceremony and reception, and AI technologies can significantly enhance this process through real-time tracking and coordination.

When planning transportation, account for the number of people needing rides, their pick-up locations, and arrival timings. The wedding party often requires special attention, with dedicated vehicles to ensure they arrive together and on schedule. Guests might need shuttle services, especially if the venue is remote or has limited parking. Advanced planning helps prevent delays and ensures a smooth flow of events.

AI technologies revolutionize transportation logistics for weddings. AI-powered ride-sharing platforms like **Uber** or **Lyft** provide on-demand transportation for guests, ensuring they can request rides as needed without pre-arranged schedules. These platforms offer real-time tracking, allowing guests to see exactly when their ride will arrive. AI-driven fleet management systems, like **Ridecell** or **Fleet Complete**, optimize routes and predict traffic patterns.

On the wedding day, these systems monitor vehicles in real-time, providing updates to the wedding planner and dynamically adjusting routes to avoid congestion. Apps like **Moovit** or **Citymapper** can guide guests through their journey, ensuring they reach the venue without confusion. By leveraging AI for real-time tracking and coordination, wedding planners can handle transportation logistics smoothly, enhancing the overall guest experience and allowing everyone to focus on enjoying the special day.

Managing Day-of Logistics with AI Technology

Effective management of day-of logistics is crucial for a smooth wedding. This involves key tasks such as setting up and breaking down venues, overseeing vendor arrivals and departures, and ensuring seamless transitions between events. Using AI technology can significantly enhance the efficiency and coordination of these tasks.

Setting up and breaking down venues requires meticulous planning. On the wedding day, setup typically begins early with tasks like arranging chairs and tables, setting up decorations, and organizing audiovisual equipment. AI technology can streamline this process using intelligent scheduling and task management with the help of apps like **Trello** and **Asana**. Enhanced with AI, these tools create detailed setup checklists, assign tasks, and send automated reminders to ensure timely completion.

After the event, AI-driven logistics apps optimize the breakdown process by tracking inventory and ensuring nothing is overlooked, making the disassembly of decorations and packing up equipment efficient and thorough. One AI-driven logistics app that optimizes the breakdown process after an event is **Rentman**. It is designed to manage event inventory and logistics, tracking all items used during the event and ensuring that everything is accounted for during the disassembly and packing up process. This makes the post-event breakdown efficient and thorough, minimizing the risk of overlooking any equipment or decorations.

Overseeing vendor arrivals and departures is another critical aspect. Vendors, such as caterers, florists, photographers, and musicians, must adhere to a strict schedule. AI-powered platforms like **EventBots** provide real-time updates on vendor locations and arrival times, using machine learning to predict and alert coordinators of potential delays, allowing for proactive adjustments. These tools can also track and confirm vendor check-outs, ensuring a smooth wrap-up.

Ensuring smooth transitions between events is essential for maintaining the flow of the wedding day. This includes coordinating shifts from the ceremony to the cocktail hour and from the cocktail hour to the reception. AI technology assists with predictive analytics to optimize transition timings. Platforms like **AllSeated** create 3D floor plans and simulate guest flow, helping planners visualize and adjust setups for each stage of the event. AI provides real-time monitoring of guest movements and sends alerts to coordinators when it's time to initiate transitions, ensuring guests are guided smoothly from one part of the event to the next.

By integrating AI technology into the planning and execution of day-of logistics, wedding planners can ensure tasks are handled efficiently and smoothly, allowing the couple and their guests to enjoy a seamless and memorable celebration free from logistical stress.

Now, let's turn our attention to contingency planning, which is essential for addressing unforeseen challenges and ensuring the wedding day proceeds seamlessly despite any unexpected occurrences.

Using AI to Anticipate and Manage Potential Issues

AI technology plays a pivotal role in enhancing contingency planning by anticipating and managing potential issues. AI-powered tools can analyze data and predict potential risks based on various factors, such as weather forecasts, vendor reliability, and logistical constraints. For example, apps like **IBM's Weather** Company can provide real-time weather updates and forecasts, allowing planners to make informed decisions about whether to move an outdoor event indoors.

AI-driven platforms like **Eventbrite** or **Zkipster** can track vendor reliability and send alerts if there are signs of potential delays or cancellations, enabling planners to arrange for substitutes in advance.

AI can also assist in managing logistics. Tools like **SmartPlan**, which uses AI to optimize event schedules and logistics, can create dynamic plans that automatically adjust in response to real-time changes. If a vendor is running late, the system can suggest alternative timelines or recommend substitute vendors. AI chatbots can also be deployed to communicate with guests, providing real-time updates on any changes to the schedule or venue, thus keeping everyone informed and reducing anxiety.

Tips for Staying Calm and Adaptable

Staying calm and adaptable in the face of unexpected challenges is crucial for successfully managing a wedding. Here are some tips:

Stay Organized: Keep all important information, such as contact details for vendors, schedules, and contingency plans, easily accessible.

Delegate Tasks: Do not try to manage everything yourself. Delegate responsibilities to trusted team members or family members to ensure that all aspects are covered and you have support when addressing issues.

Communicate Clearly: Maintain open lines of communication with the wedding party, vendors, and guests. Inform them about backup plans in advance so everyone knows what to expect if changes occur.

Practice Flexibility: Embrace the possibility of change and be prepared to make quick decisions. Flexibility is key to adapting to new situations without feeling overwhelmed.

Focus on the Big Picture: Remember that the primary goal is to celebrate the union of the couple. Minor hiccups are less significant in the grand scheme of things, so keep the focus on enjoying the day.

Utilize Technology: Leverage AI tools and mobile apps to stay informed and manage real-time changes efficiently. These technologies can reduce the burden of manual adjustments and provide peace of mind.

By having robust backup plans, leveraging AI technology to anticipate and manage issues, and maintaining a calm and adaptable approach, wedding planners can ensure that any unexpected challenges are handled with grace and efficiency. This allows the couple and their guests to enjoy a beautiful and memorable celebration, regardless of any unforeseen events.

Let's now see how these technologies are applied in real-life wedding scenarios.

Real-Life Successful AI Integration in Wedding Planning

Sarah and David, a couple planning their wedding in Los Angeles, utilized an AI-powered wedding planning platform called **Joy** to orchestrate their special day. **Joy** played a pivotal role in several aspects of their wedding planning journey: Sarah and David leveraged **Joy's** AI capabilities to streamline vendor selection. The platform analyzed their preferences, budget constraints, and venue requirements to recommend a curated list of photographers, florists, and caterers known for their quality service and compatibility with the couple's style.

Guest List Management: **Joy** integrated seamlessly with Sarah and David's wedding website and social media profiles, allowing guests to RSVP online. The AI tool managed the guest list dynamically, tracking responses in real-time, organizing seating arrangements based on guest preferences and relationships, and sending automated reminders to ensure timely responses.

Design Assistance: Sarah used **Joy** to upload inspiration photos and share her design preferences. **Joy's** AI analyzed these inputs to generate personalized mood boards and color schemes that aligned perfectly with the couple's chosen wedding theme. This streamlined decisions on décor, floral arrangements, and attire, ensuring a cohesive and visually appealing event.

Budget Optimization: **Joy's** financial tools provided Sarah and David with real-time budget tracking and optimization suggestions. The AI alerted them to potential overspending, identified areas where cost savings were possible, and proposed alternative options without compromising their vision for the wedding.

Alicia Hernandez-Whyle

Day-of Coordination: On the wedding day, **Joy's** AI managed timelines and communicated seamlessly with vendors. It provided Sarah and David with a detailed digital checklist encompassing all aspects of the event, from ceremony logistics to reception setup. This ensured that every detail was executed flawlessly, allowing the couple to enjoy their day without stress.

Post-Wedding Insights: After the celebration, **Joy** collected feedback from guests and vendors through surveys and reviews. The AI analyzed this data to provide Sarah and David with valuable insights into what aspects of the wedding were successful and areas for potential improvement. This feedback is important for future events or recommending vendors to friends or family.

Sarah and David's experience with **Joy** exemplifies how AI-powered wedding planning platforms can enhance efficiency, personalization, and overall satisfaction for couples organizing their special day.

In conclusion, the incorporation of AI technology into wedding day logistics marks a transformative leap in the landscape of wedding planning, revolutionizing how couples and planners approach the orchestration of their special day. AI's role extends beyond mere automation; it serves as a strategic ally, enabling the creation of meticulously crafted timelines that adapt dynamically to unforeseen circumstances. By analyzing vast amounts of data, AI tools anticipate potential issues and provide proactive solutions, ensuring a smooth and stress-free experience for all involved.

Moreover, AI enhances communication and coordination among vendors, ensuring everyone is aligned with the timeline and any adjustments are promptly communicated. This not only streamlines logistics but also enhances the overall guest experience, fostering an atmosphere of seamless elegance and enjoyment.

Alicia Hernandez-Whyle

Chapter Twelve

Photography and Videography: Capturing Memories with AI

One of the most significant advantages of incorporating technology into wedding planning is its ability to capture and preserve memories in ways that were previously unachievable. Advanced photography and videography tools, enhanced by artificial intelligence (AI), offer couples the opportunity to document their special day with unparalleled precision and creativity. From AI-driven photographer selection to automated editing and innovative filming techniques, technology ensures that every moment is beautifully and accurately captured.

In this chapter, we will delve into the specifics of using AI for photography and videography, including the selection of talented professionals, automated editing, and innovative filming methods.

Photography and Videography: AI-Captured Memories

Capturing the magic of a wedding day through photography and videography is essential. Selecting the right photographer and videographer is a crucial step in ensuring that the special moments of a wedding are captured beautifully.

The integration of AI into this process can significantly enhance the quality and efficiency of selecting the right professionals and planning the perfect shots.

Several AI-driven tools and platforms specialize in identifying and recommending top-rated photographers and videographers. These tools aggregate data from multiple sources, including social media, review sites, and portfolios, to create comprehensive profiles of potential candidates. For example, platforms like

Snappr use AI to evaluate photographers based on criteria such as image quality, artistic style, budget and customer feedback. This detailed analysis helps couples make informed decisions, ensuring they select professionals who can deliver high-quality results.

Once the perfect photographer and videographer are selected, the next step is to plan and schedule the shots.

Shot Planning and Scheduling with AI Assistance

Planning the perfect shots for a wedding requires careful coordination and a clear vision. AI can assist in this process by providing tools that help with shot planning and scheduling. AI-powered apps like **ShotHotspot** can suggest ideal locations and angles for photos based on the wedding venue and time of day. These apps use algorithms to analyze factors such as lighting conditions, popular photography spots, and the layout of the venue to recommend the best shots.

Additionally, AI can streamline the scheduling process by creating detailed timelines that ensure every important moment is captured without disrupting the flow of the day. Tools like **WeddingHappy** and **Joy** offer AI-driven scheduling features that coordinate with the wedding timeline, ensuring that photographers and videographers are in the right place at the right time. This allows for a seamless integration of photography and videography into the overall wedding plan, reducing stress for the couple and the planning team.

After capturing the moments, the post-production phase is where AI can make a significant impact by automating and enhancing the editing process.

Automated Editing and Enhancement Tools

The post-production phase of wedding photography and videography is where the raw footage and images are transformed into polished, professional memories. AI-powered post-production software has revolutionized this process by automating many of the time-consuming tasks traditionally handled by human editors. These advanced tools use machine learning algorithms to enhance photos and videos, ensuring consistent quality and style.

AI-powered software such as **Adobe Photoshop** and **Lightroom** for photos and **Adobe Premiere Pro** and **Final Cut Pro** for videos incorporate AI features to assist with tasks like color correction, noise reduction, and image sharpening. These tools can analyze the content of each photo or video clip and make intelligent adjustments to improve their visual appeal. By leveraging AI, these programs can produce high-quality results with less manual intervention, allowing editors to focus on creative decisions rather than technical details.

Let's delve deeper into how AI technology significantly streamlines the editing process by offering automated enhancements.

Automated Enhancements for Streamlined Editing

AI technology significantly streamlines the editing process by offering automated enhancements that save time and ensure consistency across all media. Automated tools can handle bulk edits, apply filters, and make corrections with precision, which is especially useful when dealing with large volumes of wedding photos and videos. For instance, AI can automatically adjust exposure, contrast, and white balance across an entire photo album, ensuring a uniform look and feel.

One of the standout features of AI in post-production is its ability to perform complex tasks such as object removal and background replacement. Tools like **Luminar AI** and **Skylum's** AI-based software can identify and remove unwanted elements from photos, replacing them with contextually appropriate backgrounds. This can be particularly useful for wedding photos where distractions or imperfections need to be seamlessly edited out.

To better understand the impact of AI, here are some popular AI-powered editing tools and their benefits.

AI Editing Tools and Their Benefits

Several AI-powered editing tools have become popular among wedding photographers and videographers due to their efficiency and advanced capabilities. Here are a few notable examples:

Adobe Photoshop and Lightroom: These industry-standard tools now incorporate **Adobe Sensei**, an AI platform that enhances the editing process with features like automated tagging, content-aware fill, and intelligent cropping. **Adobe Sensei** helps photographers quickly organize and edit large batches of photos, making the post-production workflow more efficient.

Luminar AI: Known for its powerful AI capabilities, **Luminar AI** offers features such as Sky Replacement, Portrait Enhancer, and AI Structure. These tools allow photographers to make dramatic improvements to photos with minimal effort, enhancing skies, retouching portraits, and adding depth and clarity to images automatically.

Final Cut Pro X: Apple's video editing software uses machine learning to analyze footage and automatically apply adjustments like color balancing and noise reduction. The software's Smart Conform feature uses AI to intelligently reframe video clips for different aspect ratios, ensuring that the most important parts of the footage remain in focus.

Magisto: This AI-powered video editing tool simplifies the creation of highlight reels and wedding videos by automatically selecting the best footage, applying transitions, and adding music. **Magisto** uses AI to analyze the emotional content of videos and photos, creating engaging and cohesive narratives with minimal manual input.

Topaz Labs: This suite of AI-powered tools includes **Gigapixel** AI for image upscaling, **DeNoise** AI for noise reduction, and **Sharpen** AI for improving image clarity. These tools are particularly useful for enhancing the quality of wedding photos taken in challenging lighting conditions or at high ISO settings.

By leveraging these AI-powered editing tools, wedding photographers and videographers can significantly reduce the time and effort required for post-production. The result is a more efficient workflow that delivers consistent, high-quality results, allowing couples to enjoy beautifully polished memories of their special day.

Another fascinating aspect of modern wedding photography and videography is the use of drones for capturing breathtaking aerial perspectives.

Utilizing Drones for Photography and Videography

Drones have revolutionized wedding photography and videography by providing breathtaking aerial perspectives that were previously unattainable. These unmanned aerial vehicles (UAVs) are equipped with high-resolution cameras, enabling photographers and videographers to capture stunning overhead shots of the ceremony, reception, and surrounding landscapes.

Using drones, wedding photographers can create dynamic and cinematic footage that adds a unique dimension to the wedding album and video. Drones can capture sweeping shots of the venue, the couple's arrival, and the entire guest assembly, offering a grand and comprehensive view of the event. Additionally, drones are ideal for capturing outdoor weddings held in picturesque locations, such as beaches, gardens, and vineyards, highlighting the natural beauty of the surroundings.

Incorporating 360-Degree Cameras for Immersive Wedding Footage

360-degree cameras provide an immersive experience that allows viewers to feel as though they are part of the wedding. These cameras capture footage in all directions, creating interactive videos that can be explored using VR headsets or through interactive platforms on computers and mobile devices.

By incorporating 360-degree cameras into wedding videography, couples can offer their guests a unique way to relive the day. For instance, a 360-degree video of the ceremony allows viewers to look around the venue and experience the event from multiple angles, as if they were present. This technology is particularly beneficial for guests who could not attend the wedding in person, providing them with an engaging and comprehensive viewing experience.

Cutting-Edge Tech for Unique Visuals

Beyond drones and 360-degree cameras, several other innovative technologies are enhancing wedding photography and videography:

Time-lapse Photography: Time-lapse photography compresses hours of footage into a few minutes, creating a visually striking effect that captures the essence of the day. This technique is perfect for documenting the setup of the venue, the flow of guests, and the transition from day to night.

GoPro Cameras: GoPro cameras, known for their durability and wide-angle capabilities, can be used to capture unique perspectives. These cameras can be attached to various objects, such as bouquets or centerpieces, to provide candid and creative footage.

Robot Photographers: Some companies now offer robot photographers, which use AI to autonomously navigate the venue and capture photos and videos. These robots can move seamlessly among guests, capturing moments from angles that a human photographer might miss.

Augmented Reality (AR) Photo Booths: AR photo booths add a layer of digital interaction to traditional photo booths. Guests can take photos with virtual props and backgrounds, creating fun and memorable images that are instantly shareable on social media.

Slow Motion Video Booths: Slow motion booths capture high-definition footage at high frame rates, allowing guests to record videos that play back in dramatic slow motion. This adds a fun and dynamic element to the wedding reception, producing videos that are both entertaining and memorable.

By embracing these cutting-edge technologies, couples can ensure that their wedding photography and videography stand out, providing unique and memorable visual experiences that capture the magic of their special day.

Next, we will discuss how live streaming enables couples to extend their wedding day beyond physical boundaries, allowing distant loved ones to witness and celebrate the event in real time.

Live Streaming Your Wedding

Live streaming has become an increasingly popular option for weddings, allowing couples to share their special day with friends and family who cannot attend in person. Setting up a live stream involves several steps to ensure that the broadcast is smooth, high-quality, and accessible to all intended viewers.

Selecting a reliable streaming platform for your wedding is crucial. Couples should choose a platform that best suits their audience's needs and technological comfort level.

Moreover, securing the right equipment is also essential to successfully live stream any event. A high-quality camera, a stable internet connection, and proper audio equipment will significantly enhance the viewing experience. Many couples opt to hire professional videographers who specialize in live streaming, ensuring that the technical aspects are handled expertly.

In addition, to make the live stream accessible, it's important to inform guests well in advance. Send out digital invitations with clear instructions on how to access the live stream, including links and any necessary passwords. Consider setting up a dedicated webpage or event on the chosen platform to provide a centralized location for information and access.

Next, we'll discuss the various platforms and tools available to make live streaming your wedding a seamless experience.

Platforms and Tools for Live Streaming

Several platforms and tools are specifically designed to facilitate live streaming for weddings, each offering unique features and capabilities:

YouTube Live: A widely accessible platform that supports high-definition streaming and offers features like live chat, allowing guests to interact during the event. It is easy to set up and provides a reliable streaming experience.

Facebook Live: Ideal for reaching a large audience, **Facebook** Live allows couples to stream directly to their friends and followers. It includes features like reactions and comments, making the experience interactive for remote guests.

Zoom: A popular choice for virtual events, **Zoom** offers robust features such as screen sharing, breakout rooms, and participant management. It is especially useful for smaller, more intimate virtual gatherings where interaction is encouraged.

Vimeo: Known for its high-quality streaming capabilities, **Vimeo** provides advanced features such as password protection, customizable viewing experiences, and detailed analytics. It is a great option for couples looking for a professional and secure streaming service.

Twitch: Originally designed for gaming, **Twitch** has expanded to include live streaming for various events. Its interactive features, such as live chat and emotes, can make the wedding live stream more engaging for viewers.

StreamYard: A user-friendly platform that integrates with multiple streaming services like **YouTube, Facebook**, and **LinkedIn**. **StreamYard** allows for easy branding, guest invites, and on-screen comments, making it a versatile tool for live streaming weddings.

By leveraging these platforms and tools, couples can ensure that their wedding live stream is high-quality, stable, and engaging for remote guests.

AI enhancements further elevate the experience, providing real-time improvements to video and audio quality, making the virtual celebration as close to the real thing as possible.

Using AI to Enhance Real-Time Video Quality

AI technology can play a significant role in enhancing the quality and stability of live streams. AI-driven video enhancement tools can automatically adjust settings such as brightness, contrast, and color balance in real time, ensuring optimal video quality regardless of changing lighting conditions.

AI can also help stabilize video feeds, reducing the effects of camera shake and movement. Tools like **NVIDIA's** AI-powered video enhancement software use machine learning algorithms to analyze the video feed and make real-time adjustments, providing a smoother viewing experience.

Additionally, AI can be used to manage bandwidth and optimize streaming quality based on the viewer's internet connection. Adaptive bitrate streaming, powered by AI, adjusts the video quality dynamically to match the available bandwidth, minimizing buffering and ensuring a continuous stream.

Lastly, seamless coordination between different aspects of the wedding is crucial for a cohesive and well-executed event.

Coordinating Photography, Videography, and Reception

Seamless coordination between different aspects of the wedding, such as photography, videography, and reception planning, is crucial for a cohesive and well-executed event. AI-driven scheduling tools like **HoneyBook** and **Dubsado** can automate the process of coordinating with various vendors, ensuring that everyone is aware of the timeline and any changes.

For example, tools like **WedSites** and **Timeline Genius** can manage the schedules of photographers and videographers, ensuring they are present at key moments without disrupting the flow of events. **WedSites** offers real-time coordination, helping to synchronize the timing of different activities, such as the first dance, cake cutting, and speeches. Meanwhile, **Timeline Genius** ensures that all photographers and videographers are well prepared and in position to capture these moments, providing a seamless experience throughout the wedding day.

In closing, utilizing AI in wedding photography and videography represents a remarkable leap in how we capture and preserve memories. AI-driven tools and technologies offer unprecedented levels of precision, creativity, and efficiency, ensuring that every special moment is beautifully documented. From selecting top-rated photographers and videographers to planning the perfect shots and utilizing automated editing tools, AI simplifies and enhances the entire process.

Advanced technologies such as drones, 360-degree cameras, and live streaming platforms provide unique perspectives and interactive experiences that elevate the wedding day for both the couple and their guests. By leveraging these innovations, couples

Alicia Hernandez-Whyle

can create a wedding album and video that are not only visually stunning but also immersive and memorable.

As technology continues to advance, the possibilities for enhancing and preserving these cherished memories will only expand, offering couples innovative ways to relive and share their love story for years to come.

Chapter Thirteen

Entertainment and Music: Creating the Perfect Ambience

Music plays a crucial role in weddings, serving as the emotional backdrop that enhances the significance of each moment. From the first note of the prelude to the last dance at the reception, music sets the tone and creates an atmosphere that resonates with both the couple and their guests. Its emotional impact cannot be overstated; music has the power to evoke memories, stir deep emotions, and foster a sense of unity and celebration.

Understanding the emotional significance of music at a wedding allows for more thoughtful selection of the playlist, ensuring each song enhances the experience. Key moments that require music include the ceremony, reception, and special dances. During the ceremony, music often accompanies the entrance of the bridal party, the bride's walk down the aisle, and significant moments like the exchange of vows and rings. Each piece selected should reflect the gravity and beauty of the occasion.

At the reception, music transitions from solemnity to celebration. Background music during dinner, upbeat tracks to get guests dancing, and the first dance song are all crucial elements contributing to the event's flow and enjoyment. Special dances, such as the father-daughter dance and mother-son dance, also require careful song selection to ensure they are poignant and memorable. Thoughtfully selecting music for these key moments makes the wedding a seamless and emotionally rich experience for all involved.

How AI Compiles the Perfect Playlist

AI music curation tools leverage advanced algorithms and machine learning technologies to create customized playlists for specific events and preferences. These tools analyze data such as song characteristics, historical user preferences, and contextual information to generate playlists that match the desired mood and theme of an event. Popular platforms like **Spotify**, **Apple Music**, and **Deezer** use natural language processing (NLP) to understand user inputs and sentiment analysis to gauge emotional responses to different types of music.

Additionally, AI systems employ collaborative filtering, which recommends music based on similar user preferences, and content-based filtering, which suggests tracks with similar acoustic properties.

For weddings, AI selection tools are particularly effective as they can analyze and incorporate the couple's musical tastes, cultural traditions, and the overall theme of the wedding. By integrating these elements, AI ensures the music selection is both personal and appropriate, creating a unique and memorable atmosphere. Moreover, advancements in deep learning and neural networks are enabling even more sophisticated and accurate music recommendations.

Alicia Hernandez-Whyle

Customizing Playlists Based on Preferences and Themes

One of the primary advantages of using AI for music playlist selection is its ability to customize playlists based on specific preferences, themes, and guest demographics. By inputting detailed information about the couple's favorite genres, artists, and songs, AI tools can generate a playlist that aligns with their personal tastes. Additionally, specifying the theme of the wedding, whether classic, rustic, beach, or modern, allows the AI to select music that complements the chosen theme.

AI tools like **DJ Intelligence** and **Vibo** are particularly effective in this regard. **DJ Intelligence** allows couples to input their musical preferences and wedding theme, then generates a tailored playlist that perfectly matches their vision. **Vibo**, on the other hand, provides an interactive platform where couples can collaborate with their DJ to refine the playlist, ensuring it reflects both their style and the diverse tastes of their guests.

These AI tools also consider guest demographics, ensuring the playlist appeals to a wide range of ages and cultural backgrounds. For instance, if a wedding has a diverse guest list, the AI can include a mix of contemporary hits, timeless classics, and culturally significant songs that resonate with different groups. This level of customization helps create an inclusive and enjoyable experience for everyone attending the wedding.

To further enhance the playlist, AI tools can analyze the timing and flow of the wedding day. They can select softer, more romantic songs for the ceremony and dinner while opting for upbeat, energetic tracks for the dance floor. This ensures that the music transitions seamlessly throughout the event, maintaining the desired atmosphere at each stage.

Real-Time Adjustments to Playlists During the Event

One of the most impressive capabilities of AI music curation is its ability to make real-time adjustments to playlists during the event. Using sensors and feedback mechanisms, AI systems can monitor the energy and mood of the crowd and adjust the music accordingly. For example, if the AI detects that the dance floor is emptying, it might switch to a more popular, high-energy song to entice guests back to dancing. Conversely, if it senses that the crowd is getting tired, it may choose to slow down the tempo to give guests a break.

Some advanced AI tools are equipped with facial recognition and motion detection technologies, allowing them to gauge the emotional responses of guests and adapt the playlist in real-time. This dynamic adjustment ensures that the music always aligns with the current mood and energy of the event, creating a continuously engaging and enjoyable experience.

Furthermore, AI can accommodate spontaneous requests and changes in the schedule. If a special moment arises that wasn't planned, such as a surprise performance, the AI can seamlessly integrate the necessary adjustments without disrupting the flow of the event. This level of flexibility and responsiveness is invaluable in ensuring that the wedding remains smooth and memorable.

Weddings Enhanced by AI Music Compilation

Emma and Raj hosted a multicultural wedding in New York City, blending Western and Indian traditions. They wanted a playlist that reflected their diverse backgrounds and appealed to their guests, who ranged from older relatives with traditional tastes to younger friends who preferred contemporary hits. By using an AI music curation tool, they were able to create a seamless blend of Bollywood classics, Western pop songs, and timeless love ballads.

Soundtrack Your Brand analyzed the couple's favorite artists and genres and incorporated suggestions based on the demographic data provided. During the ceremony, traditional Indian instrumental music played softly in the background, enhancing the solemnity of the occasion. For the reception, the playlist transitioned smoothly from romantic slow dances to high energy tracks that filled the dance floor.

The AI's ability to adapt in real-time was particularly beneficial when the couple's parents requested traditional songs on the spot, ensuring that the cultural significance was honored without missing a beat.

Stunning Lighting and Effects

AI-driven lighting systems are revolutionizing event lighting design, offering unprecedented control and customization. These systems use artificial intelligence to analyze various aspects of the event and dynamically adjust lighting to enhance the overall atmosphere. AI lighting tools, such as **Philips Hue** and **LIFX**, can create a wide range of effects, from subtle ambiance enhancements to dramatic visual spectacles. These systems integrate with event management software, allowing for seamless control and real-time adjustments.

For weddings, AI lighting systems can be customized to match the mood and theme of the event. This means creating a lighting scheme that complements the decor, enhances key moments, and creates the desired ambiance. Tools like **Chauvet DJ** and **Astera's Titan Tubes** use AI algorithms to analyze the wedding's theme, color scheme, and timeline. By inputting details such as the couple's favorite colors, the overall aesthetic, and specific moments (like the first dance or cake cutting), these tools can generate a tailored lighting plan.

For instance, during a romantic outdoor wedding, AI-driven lights can softly illuminate the venue with warm hues, transitioning to more vibrant colors as the evening progresses and the celebration kicks into high gear. During the ceremony, the lighting can be programmed to subtly shift in color temperature, enhancing the emotional impact of vows and speeches.

Dynamic Lighting Changes During the Event

One of the standout features of AI lighting systems is their ability to make dynamic changes during the event. Using sensors and real-time data, AI tools can adjust lighting based on factors like the time of day, the energy level of the crowd, and specific cues in the event timeline. For example, systems like **Martin**

Professional's M-Series and the **GrandMA3** from MA Lighting can react to music beats, speeches, or significant moments, altering the lighting to match the mood and energy.

During the reception, if the AI detects an uptick in energy on the dance floor, it can respond by intensifying the lights, using strobe effects, or making color changes to enhance the party atmosphere. Conversely, for quieter moments, such as a toast or an intimate slow dance, the lighting can automatically soften and focus to create a more personal and touching environment.

Visual Effects and Projections

AI technology can also be used to create immersive visual effects that transform the wedding venue. Tools such as **Resolume** and **TouchDesigner** enable the creation of stunning visual displays that can be projected onto various surfaces, enhancing the overall aesthetic and providing unique experiences for guests. These tools use AI to analyze the event space and create visuals perfectly mapped to the venue's architecture.

For example, during the reception, AI can project moving patterns, floral designs, or videos that reflect the couple's journey together. These projections can change in real-time, reacting to the music or specific moments in the event, creating a dynamic and immersive environment that captivates guests.

Projection mapping, enhanced by AI, is a powerful technique used to create visually stunning experiences. This technology involves projecting images or videos onto irregularly shaped surfaces, turning them into dynamic displays. AI tools like **Lightform** and **MadMapper** precisely map these projections, ensuring they align perfectly with the physical contours of the venue.

In weddings, projection mapping can be used in various ways. For instance, during the reception, the walls of the venue can be transformed into a starry night sky, a beautiful garden, or any other theme that matches the couple's vision. Even the wedding cake can be a canvas for projection mapping, displaying animated designs that change throughout the evening. This not only adds a wow factor but also creates memorable photo opportunities for guests.

AI-Enhanced Lighting: Real-Life Examples

Sophia and Liam wanted a fairytale-themed wedding, complete with magical lighting effects. Using the Philips Hue AI-driven lighting system, their event planner created a dynamic lighting plan that shifted throughout the day.

During the ceremony, the lighting was soft and warm, with hues of pink and gold. As the night progressed, the lights transitioned to cooler blues and purples, creating an enchanting, dream-like atmosphere.

The AI system also synchronized the lights with the couple's first dance, enhancing the moment with gentle, twinkling lights that made it feel like they were dancing under a sky full of stars.

Evolution of Traditional Photo Booths to AI-Enhanced Versions

Traditional photo booths have long been a staple at weddings, providing guests with a fun and memorable activity. However, the integration of AI technology has revolutionized these booths, transforming them into interactive experiences that offer much more than just simple photo strips. AI-enhanced photo booths come equipped with advanced cameras and software that can recognize faces, apply digital enhancements, and create personalized photo experiences in real-time. These booths can automatically adjust lighting, suggest poses, and even animate photos, providing a dynamic and engaging experience for guests.

Alicia Hernandez-Whyle

Modern AI enhanced photo booths offer a plethora of features designed to enhance the guest experience. Digital props and filters allow guests to customize their photos with fun and creative elements, such as virtual hats, glasses, and themed backgrounds. These features provide endless possibilities for personalization, similar to those found on popular social media platforms.

Another significant advancement is the ability to instantly share photos. AI-enhanced photo booths can be connected to social media accounts, enabling guests to post their photos directly from the booth. This instant sharing capability not only adds to the fun but also helps spread the joy of the event in real-time. Additionally, guests can receive digital copies of their photos via email or text, ensuring they have a lasting memento of the special day.

Virtual Reality Experiences

Virtual reality (VR) technology offers exciting opportunities to entertain guests at weddings. By incorporating VR, couples can provide immersive experiences that transport guests to different worlds or allow them to participate in interactive activities. One popular application is virtual tours. For destination weddings or couples with significant places in their love story, VR can offer guests a chance to explore these locations in a fully immersive way, even if they can't be physically present.

In addition to tours, VR can be used to offer a variety of games and interactive experiences. Guests can compete in virtual dance-offs, explore fantasy worlds, or participate in collaborative challenges.

These experiences can be tailored to match the wedding theme, creating a cohesive and engaging atmosphere.

Integrating Virtual Reality (VR) into the Wedding Theme

Integrating VR into the wedding theme and decor can create a seamless and immersive experience for guests. For example, a couple having a fairytale-themed wedding might use VR to transport guests to a magical forest or castle. The VR setup can be designed to blend with the physical decor, enhancing the overall ambiance of the event. Strategic placement of VR stations around the venue ensures that guests have easy access to these experiences without disrupting the flow of the wedding.

To make the VR experience more personal, couples can create custom content that reflects their journey and relationship. This might include a virtual tour of significant locations, a recreation of their proposal, or a virtual storybook of their relationship milestones. By incorporating these personalized elements, couples can create a unique and memorable experience for their guests.

Augmented Reality (AR) Features

Augmented Reality (AR) offers a new dimension to photo opportunities and guest interactions at weddings. AR technology can overlay digital elements onto the physical world, creating interactive and engaging experiences. For example, couples can set up AR photo stations where guests can pose with virtual characters, effects, or themed backgrounds seamlessly integrated into the real world. These AR photo opportunities can be tailored to match the wedding theme, adding a unique and playful element to the event.

Beyond photos, AR can facilitate interactive guest activities. For instance, guests can participate in AR scavenger hunts around the venue, where they find and interact with virtual objects or clues. This not only entertains guests but also encourages them to explore and engage with the wedding environment in a fun and interactive way.

Custom AR Filters and Effects for a Personal Touch

Custom AR filters and effects provide a personalized touch that enhances the guest experience. Similar to the filters available on social media platforms like Instagram and Snapchat, these custom AR effects can reflect the couple's personality, wedding theme, or significant moments in their relationship. Guests can use these filters to take photos or videos that are uniquely branded for the wedding, creating personalized keepsakes and shareable content.

Couples can work with developers to create bespoke AR effects, such as virtual fireworks, thematic overlays, or animated elements that react to guests' movements. These custom AR features add a modern and tech-savvy element to the wedding, creating memorable and interactive experiences that guests will talk about long after the event.

In summary, incorporating interactive technologies like AI-enhanced photo booths, VR experiences, and AR features significantly enhances the guest experience at weddings. These technologies offer personalized, engaging, and memorable activities that align with the wedding theme and create lasting impressions. As technology continues to evolve, the possibilities for creating unique and immersive wedding experiences will only expand, offering couples new ways to celebrate their special day with their loved ones.

Alicia Hernandez-Whyle

Interactive Entertainment Options

AI-powered games offer unique and engaging ways to entertain wedding guests, making the event more interactive and memorable. These games can be customized to fit the wedding theme, the couple's interests, and the demographics of the guests. Popular AI tools such as **Kahoot** and **TriviaMaker** are ideal for creating fun and personalized gaming experiences.

Trivia Games

Trivia games are a fantastic way to entertain guests and test their knowledge about the couple or general topics. Using platforms like **Kahoot**, couples can create custom trivia games with questions about their relationship, wedding theme, or general knowledge that relates to their interests. The AI within **Kahoot** helps generate a variety of questions and ensures a smooth, engaging gameplay experience.

Treasure Hunts

Treasure hunts can be made more exciting with AI tools like **GooseChase**, which allows couples to design scavenger hunts throughout the wedding venue. The AI in **GooseChase** creates dynamic challenges and clues based on the wedding's layout and theme, guiding guests to different locations and tasks. This not only entertains but also encourages guests to explore the venue and interact with each other.

Personalized Quizzes

Personalized quizzes are another engaging option. AI tools like **TriviaMaker** offer the capability to create custom quizzes that reflect the couple's story and preferences. Guests can participate via their smartphones, and the AI dynamically adjusts the difficulty and content based on real-time feedback and participation levels.

AI-Driven Music Playlists and Karaoke

AI-driven music playlists and karaoke sessions, using tools like **DJ Pro AI**, provide continuous entertainment. This tool analyzes guests' music preferences and generates playlists to keep the dance floor active. For karaoke, **VocalTune** AI suggests songs based on the singers' vocal range and preferences, ensuring a fun and inclusive experience.

As we conclude, advanced technologies such as AI and AR in wedding planning can transform a traditional celebration into an unforgettable experience. From curating the perfect music playlist to creating dynamic lighting and visual effects, AI-driven tools

Alicia Hernandez-Whyle

offer unparalleled customization and real-time adaptability. These technologies allow for seamless coordination and personalization, ensuring that every aspect of the wedding aligns with the couple's vision and resonates with their guests.

Chapter Fourteen

AI for Legal and Administrative Tasks

Planning a wedding involves a multitude of legal and administrative tasks that are crucial for ensuring the marriage is legally recognized and all necessary paperwork is in order. Navigating the complex legal requirements for obtaining a marriage license, changing names on official documents, and managing various other administrative responsibilities can be overwhelming for couples. Each jurisdiction has its own set of rules, paperwork, and timelines, which adds to the stress of wedding planning. Additionally, dealing with multiple government offices, filling out forms, and coordinating with different agencies often requires significant time and effort.

AI-powered tools are revolutionizing the way couples handle these legal and administrative tasks. By providing step-by-step guidance tailored to specific requirements, AI simplifies the process of obtaining a marriage license and ensures that all necessary documents are prepared accurately and on time.

These tools can offer checklists, reminders, and automated form filling, reducing the likelihood of errors and missed deadlines. AI applications can also streamline the process of name changes by generating personalized name-change packets with all the necessary forms and instructions for different agencies. This significantly reduces the time and effort required to update official documents.

Moreover, AI can help couples stay organized by managing digital copies of important documents, setting up automated reminders for upcoming deadlines, and providing access to legal resources and support. By centralizing information and offering real-time updates, AI ensures that couples are always aware of what needs to be done and when, allowing them to focus on the more enjoyable aspects of wedding planning.

While the benefits of AI in wedding planning are significant, it is important to recognize that access to these technologies may be limited in certain regions. Additionally, some couples may have concerns about the security and privacy of their personal information when using AI tools. It is crucial to choose reputable AI platforms that prioritize data protection and comply with relevant regulations. The availability and functionality of AI tools may vary by country, and some regions may not have access to these technologies or may have different application processes. Being aware of these variations and selecting tools that meet the necessary security and privacy standards is essential.

Now, let's delve into the first major legal task obtaining: a marriage license.

Obtaining a Marriage License

The requirements for obtaining a marriage license vary by jurisdiction. These can include age restrictions, waiting periods, and necessary documentation, such as birth certificates, proof of identity, or previous marriage dissolution papers. Understanding these requirements is essential for a smooth application process.

LegalZoom is a valuable tool in this context. This platform uses AI to provide customized checklists based on your location. It aggregates and updates legal requirements from different jurisdictions, ensuring you have the most accurate and up-to-date information. **LegalZoom** can also guide you through filling out the application forms, minimizing errors and omissions.

For further assistance, consider **DoNotPay**. An AI-powered virtual assistant that guides you through the process of gathering required documents and submitting applications. It can answer common questions, such as what specific documents are needed in your county or state, and help ensure that no steps are missed. It also offers a simulation feature where you can practice filling out forms to ensure accuracy before the actual submission.

After gathering the necessary documents, couples must submit an application, often at a county clerk's office or online. This process can be time-consuming and requires careful attention to detail to avoid delays.

To streamline this step, **TurboLaw** can help. This AI tool automates the filling out of forms and can schedule appointments at the nearest office. **TurboLaw** provides reminders and updates on your application status, ensuring you do not miss any important deadlines. It also offers a document verification feature that checks for completeness and accuracy before submission.

Another useful tool is **ClerkAssist**. This AI assistant can book appointments with the county clerk's office and track the application process. **ClerkAssist** can notify you of any changes or additional requirements. It can also generate a timeline of expected processing times based on current data from various clerk offices, helping you plan accordingly.

Ensuring Legal Requirements are Met

Each jurisdiction may have specific laws regarding marriage, such as blood tests, waiting periods, or officiant qualifications. Ensuring compliance with these laws is essential to avoid any legal issues.

LawGeex offers robust support in this area. This AI legal advisor reviews local laws and ensures all requirements are met. It can compare your documentation against legal standards and highlight any discrepancies. **LawGeex** also offers a comprehensive legal review feature, scanning all your submitted documents and checking them against local and state regulations.

Documentation and Record-Keeping

Proper documentation and record-keeping are crucial for legal verification and future reference. Ensuring that all paperwork is in order and securely stored can prevent future legal complications.

DocuSign is an excellent tool for this purpose. An AI-powered electronic signature tool, **DocuSign** ensures all necessary documents are signed and stored securely. It provides a legal audit trail and easy access to all your documents. **DocuSign** also offers a workflow automation feature that routes documents to the correct parties for signatures in the proper order.

Another effective solution is **FileInvite**. This tool uses AI to collect and organize documents from various sources, ensuring all paperwork is complete and correctly filed. **FileInvite** can send automated reminders to parties who have not yet submitted their required documents, helping to keep the process on track.

Handling Name Change

Changing your name after marriage involves notifying various governmental and financial institutions, updating legal documents, and ensuring all records reflect your new name. This can be a complex and time-consuming process, but AI can simplify it significantly.

UpdateMyName is a useful AI assistant that helps update your name across multiple platforms and services. **UpdateMyName** tracks your progress and provides reminders for any pending changes. It can also integrate with your email and calendar to schedule appointments at necessary agencies and send notifications about required documents or steps.

HitchSwitch can be essential in the name change process. This AI service tracks the status of your name change requests and provides real-time updates. **HitchSwitch** ensures that all records are updated and alerts you if any further action is needed. It can also generate reports showing which changes have been completed and which are still pending.

In summary, AI into the legal and administrative tasks of wedding planning can significantly alleviate the stress and complexity involved in ensuring your marriage is legally recognized and all necessary paperwork is properly handled. From obtaining a marriage license to managing name changes, AI-powered tools provide customized guidance, streamline processes, and reduce the likelihood of errors, making these tasks more manageable and efficient.

Alicia Hernandez-Whyle

Part Five: After the Wedding

Chapter Fifteen

Post-Wedding Bliss: Preserving and Sharing Memories

The excitement of your wedding day doesn't end once the last guest has left. Instead, a new chapter begins, filled with opportunities to cherish and relive the magical moments. From organizing and editing photos and videos to expressing gratitude through thank-you notes, the post-wedding period is a blend of tasks and reflections that can be both rewarding and overwhelming.

Alicia Hernandez-Whyle

AI technology offers innovative solutions to streamline these activities, making it easier to preserve your memories and share them with loved ones. This chapter explores how AI can assist in various post-wedding tasks, ensuring that the joy of your special day extends well beyond the event itself.

One of the most exciting aspects of the post-wedding phase is sorting through the plethora of photos and videos captured during the celebration. Advanced AI tools can significantly enhance this experience by providing sophisticated editing capabilities that were once reserved for professionals. From automatic enhancements and artistic effects to creating seamless video montages, AI can transform your raw footage into beautifully polished keepsakes.

Additionally, AI-driven platforms simplify the creation and sharing of digital albums, allowing you to effortlessly compile and distribute your cherished moments to friends and family.

Beyond preserving memories, the post-wedding period involves managing a range of practical tasks, such as sending thank-you notes, handling returns, and maintaining communication with vendors and guests. AI tools can automate and personalize these processes, ensuring that every task is completed efficiently and thoughtfully. Moreover, creating and maintaining a wedding website using AI tools can serve as a lasting digital archive of your wedding journey, providing a platform to share updates, thank-yous, and highlights. By leveraging AI in these areas, you can navigate the post-wedding period with ease, leaving you more time to reflect on and enjoy the memories of your special day.

Sharing Your Special Day

Sharing your wedding memories with friends and family is simple with digital albums and social media. AI-powered platforms like **Google Photos** and **Apple Photos** can automatically organize your photos into albums based on location, date, and even facial recognition. These tools also offer features like automatic slideshow creation and photo book printing, allowing you to create physical keepsakes as well. This ensures that your memories are not only preserved digitally but also in tangible forms that can be cherished for years to come.

Social media platforms like **Instagram** and **Facebook** are enhanced with AI to optimize your posts. AI can suggest the best times to post, generate captions, and even analyze engagement metrics to help you reach a wider audience. Additionally, AI tools like **Canva** offer easy-to-use templates and design tools to create beautiful social media posts and stories. These tools can help you craft visually appealing content that captures the essence of your wedding day, making it easy to share your joy with a larger audience.

Moreover, AI can assist in managing the privacy and distribution of your digital albums and social media posts. For example, AI algorithms can detect and tag people in your photos, allowing you to share specific albums with select groups of people. This ensures that your wedding memories are shared with the right audience while maintaining privacy and security.

By leveraging AI tools for creating digital albums and sharing on social media, you can effortlessly showcase your special day and keep your loved ones engaged with your wedding journey.

AI for Building and Maintaining Your Wedding Website

A wedding website is a great way to share your journey and keep your loved ones informed. AI tools can help you build and maintain a professional-looking website with ease. Platforms like **Wix** and **Squarespace** offer AI-driven website builders that can suggest layouts, color schemes, and content based on your preferences. These tools also offer integration with social media, RSVP management, and guest book features. By using AI, you can create a personalized and engaging wedding website that serves as a hub for all your wedding-related information.

Furthermore, AI can assist in maintaining your website post-wedding by updating it with new photos, thank-you messages, and event highlights. This ensures that your wedding website remains a valuable resource and a cherished memory for you and your guests. AI-driven content management systems can automatically update and organize your website content, making it easy to share updates and keep your site fresh and relevant.

Additionally, AI tools can enhance the interactivity and functionality of your wedding website. For example, AI chatbots can provide instant responses to guest inquiries, helping them find information quickly and efficiently. AI can also analyze visitor data to help you understand which sections of your website are most popular and how to improve the user experience. By leveraging AI to build and maintain your wedding website, you can create a dynamic and engaging online presence that continues to celebrate your wedding long after the day itself.

Thank-You Notes, Returns and More

Alicia Hernandez-Whyle

Expressing gratitude and staying connected with those who helped make your wedding day special is an important part of the post-wedding experience. The post-wedding period can be filled with numerous tasks, from sending thank-you notes to handling returns. By automating thank-you notes and managing post-wedding communications, you can ensure that every guest and vendor feels appreciated and valued. AI can assist in making this process efficient and meaningful.

AI tools can streamline these processes, offering templates for personalized thank-you notes and automating the sending process. Services like **Postable** and **ThankView** allow you to customize digital and physical thank-you cards, adding personal touches while saving time. This ensures that every guest and vendor receives a thoughtful thank-you note, reflecting your appreciation for their presence and contributions to your special day.

For returns and other logistics, AI can provide reminders and track your progress, ensuring you stay organized and stress-free. Platforms like **Honeydue** and **Todoist** can help manage your to-do lists, set deadlines, and even remind you of upcoming tasks. Additionally, AI chatbots can assist with customer service inquiries for returns, making the process smoother. These tools can help you handle post-wedding responsibilities efficiently, allowing you to focus on enjoying your newlywed life.

Moreover, these AI can assist in managing and organizing the numerous gifts and donations you may receive. By using AI-driven tools, you can easily keep track of who gave what, send timely thank-you notes, and even manage exchanges or returns. This level of organization ensures that you don't overlook any details and helps you maintain a positive relationship with your guests and vendors. By utilizing AI for managing post-wedding tasks, you can ensure a smooth and stress-free transition from your wedding day to your new life together.

Tools and Templates for Personalized Messages

AI-powered tools can help you create personalized thank-you notes quickly and effortlessly. Platforms like **Handwrytten** and **Felt** offer services where AI-generated templates can be customized with personal touches. These platforms also offer options for handwriting fonts, making your notes feel more personal even when automated. This ensures that each thank-you note reflects your gratitude and appreciation in a heartfelt manner.

Additionally, AI can assist in tracking who has received thank-you notes and who hasn't, ensuring that no one is overlooked. This can be particularly useful for large weddings where keeping track of all guests and gifts can be challenging. AI tools can also help you schedule and send thank-you notes at the right time, ensuring that your messages are timely and appreciated.

Moreover, AI can help you personalize each thank-you note based on the recipient's relationship to you and their contribution to your wedding. By analyzing data from your guest list and gift registry, AI can suggest personalized messages that reflect the unique connection you have with each guest. This level of personalization ensures that every thank-you note is meaningful and sincere, strengthening your relationships with your guests and vendors.

Managing Post-Wedding Communications

Maintaining communication with your vendors and guests after the wedding can be beneficial for future events and relationships. AI can assist in managing these communications by providing reminders for follow-ups, organizing contact information, and automating messages. Tools like **HubSpot** and **Mailchimp** can help you create and send newsletters, updates, and thank-you messages to your guests and vendors. This ensures that you stay connected and maintain positive relationships with those who contributed to your special day.

For vendors, AI can help you schedule and manage follow-up meetings, review contracts, and even handle payments. This ensures that all loose ends are tied up and that you maintain positive relationships with vendors. AI tools can also help you track and analyze vendor performance, providing valuable insights for future events.

Furthermore, AI can assist in managing your social media interactions with guests and vendors. By using AI-driven tools, you can monitor and respond to comments, messages, and reviews in a timely and personalized manner. This level of engagement helps you build a supportive and connected community around your wedding, ensuring that your relationships continue to thrive long after the event.

Reflecting on Your Wedding Planning Journey

Taking time to reflect on your wedding planning journey can provide valuable insights and cherished memories. AI tools can help you compile a digital journal or scrapbook, documenting the highs and lows of your experience. Platforms like **Evernote** and Journey can help you organize your thoughts, photos, and notes into a cohesive narrative. This allows you to capture the full scope of your wedding journey, from the initial planning stages to the final celebrations.

Reflecting on your journey can also involve analyzing data from your planning process. AI can help you understand what worked well and what didn't, providing insights that can be useful for future events. This can include everything from budget management to guest satisfaction. By analyzing data from your wedding, AI can identify patterns and trends that can help you improve your planning and decision-making processes.

Moreover, reflecting on your wedding journey allows you to appreciate the effort and love that went into creating your special day. By documenting your experiences and memories, you create a lasting record that you can look back on for years to come. AI tools can help you organize and present these memories in a meaningful and engaging way, ensuring that your wedding journey is remembered and cherished.

Reviewing Vendors and Sharing Feedback

Providing feedback on your vendors can help future brides make informed decisions. AI platforms like Trustpilot and Yelp can simplify the review process, offering prompts and templates for detailed feedback. Additionally, these tools can aggregate reviews and ratings, creating a comprehensive resource for other brides. This helps build a supportive and informed community of wedding planners and couples, ensuring that everyone benefits from shared experiences.

AI can also help you share your feedback on social media and wedding planning forums. By analyzing your reviews and identifying key points, AI can help you craft posts that are both informative and engaging. This not only helps future brides but also supports vendors who provided excellent service. By sharing your experiences, you contribute to a culture of transparency and trust within the wedding industry.

Furthermore, AI can assist in managing and analyzing feedback from your own wedding. By using AI-driven tools, you can gather and interpret feedback from your guests and vendors, identifying areas for improvement and celebrating successes. This level of analysis ensures that you learn from your experiences and continue to grow and improve in your future planning endeavors.

In summary, the post-wedding period is a time to cherish memories, express gratitude, and reflect on the incredible journey of planning and celebrating your special day. By making use of AI tools, you can enhance your photo and video keepsakes, efficiently manage thank-you notes and other post-wedding tasks, and maintain meaningful connections with your guests and vendors. AI solutions ensure that your wedding day remains a treasured chapter in your life's story, celebrated and remembered for years to come.

Part Six: Real-Life Stories and Case Studies

Alicia Hernandez-Whyle

Chapter Sixteen

Success Stories: Brides Who Mastered AI in Wedding Planning

In today's ever-evolving wedding industry, the integration of artificial intelligence (AI) is transforming how brides navigate their journey from engagement to the big day. Real-life examples vividly highlight the revolutionary impact of AI, showcasing how it simplifies wedding planning by making the entire process more streamlined, enjoyable, and personalized.

This chapter showcases the success stories of brides who have used AI in their planning. These accounts reveal how AI can streamline vendor coordination, manage budgets, and create personalized experiences, reducing stress and making planning more manageable.

These firsthand stories illustrate AI's flexibility and how it can be tailored to fit unique needs. The lessons learned offer practical advice for future brides on incorporating AI into their planning.

By sharing these success stories, my intention is to demystify AI and demonstrate its potential to revolutionize wedding planning. Whether managing logistics, personalizing details, or ensuring a seamless event, AI provides solutions that enhance the joy of planning a wedding.

Now, let's dive into the insights from brides who successfully used AI in their wedding planning.

Brides' AI Success Stories

To gather the most insightful and diverse perspectives, I conducted in-depth interviews with brides who successfully integrated AI into their wedding planning. The selection criteria focused on brides who utilized a range of AI tools, represented various cultural backgrounds, and planned weddings of different styles and scales.

Each interview aimed to capture not only the practical applications of AI but also the emotional journey and unique challenges each bride faced. By presenting a comprehensive overview of their experiences, I intend to provide valuable lessons and inspiration for future brides.

Makeila's High-Tech Fairytale Wedding

Background: Makeila's Vision and Initial Challenges

Makeila had always envisioned a fairytale wedding, where every detail shimmered with perfection and her guests felt the magic she had dreamed of since she was a little girl. However, as she began the planning process, she quickly realized the complexity of the task. The countless decisions, endless coordination, and juggling it all with her demanding career became a crushing burden. Adding to her frustration was the fact that she simply couldn't afford a wedding planner. Makeila needed a solution that could help her manage everything efficiently while still allowing her to maintain a personal touch.

How AI Tools Helped: Specific Tools and Features Used

Desperate for help, Makeila turned to AI tools, hoping they could offer some relief. **WeddingWire** became her guiding light, offering personalized vendor recommendations that spared her hours of stress and automated timeline management that kept her on track. **Zola**, another AI tool, assisted her in creating a customized wedding website and managing her guest list with ease. For design inspiration and coordination, Makeila relied on **Joy**, an AI tool that helped her visualize different décor options and stay organized with checklists and reminders. These tools collectively transformed her planning experience, enabling her to focus on the creative aspects of her wedding while automating the logistical details.

Key Takeaways: Makeila's Advice for Future Brides

Reflecting on her journey, Makeila acknowledges that embracing technology was a game changer in her wedding planning process. Her key advice for future brides is to start using AI tools early, but to also recognize that these tools are not a magic fix; they require time and patience to learn. She suggests experimenting with different features to find what truly works for your needs and being realistic about the tools' capabilities. Makeila emphasizes that while AI can streamline both big-picture planning and small details, it's important to stay involved and maintain a personal touch. Most importantly, she encourages brides to view AI as a helpful support system rather than a replacement, allowing them to bring their unique vision to life while keeping stress at bay.

Anjali's Cultural Fusion Wedding

Background: Integrating Different Cultural Elements

Anjali dreamed of a wedding that would be a true reflection of the love she and her partner shared—a beautiful union of her rich Indian heritage and his deep-rooted Irish traditions. She envisioned a celebration where the vibrant colors of a traditional Hindu ceremony would harmonize with the timeless beauty of a Celtic handfasting ritual, honoring both cultures in a way that felt meaningful and authentic. But as she delved into the planning, the sheer weight of the task began to overwhelm her. How could she weave together such diverse customs, ceremonies, and rituals into a single day that felt cohesive and respectful?

The pressure of ensuring every moment was perfect, of honoring her family's traditions while embracing her partner's, was immense. Coordinating with family members from different cultural backgrounds only added to the complexity, and Anjali found herself feeling increasingly desperate for a solution. She longed for a way to manage these daunting challenges without losing the essence of what made both cultures so special, but the path forward seemed impossibly tangled.

Managing Multiple Traditions With AI

Faced with the challenge of blending her Indian heritage with her partner's Irish traditions, Anjali turned to AI tools to bring her vision to life. She relied on **The Knot**, an AI-driven wedding planning platform, which became her trusted guide in crafting a personalized planning timeline that carefully accounted for the intricate details of both the Hindu ceremony and the Celtic handfasting ritual. The platform's vendor recommendations were a game-changer, connecting her with specialists who understood the nuances of multicultural weddings and could honor the significance of each tradition.

To ensure that every guest felt respected and included, Anjali used **AllSeated**, an AI tool that allowed her to design a seating plan with precision. This tool was invaluable in helping her navigate cultural customs, such as ensuring that elders and specific family members were seated according to tradition while still creating a warm, inclusive atmosphere. The complexity of planning a fusion wedding required real-time collaboration, especially with family members spread across different regions. For this, Anjali turned to **Trello**, an AI-powered project management tool, which became

the backbone of her coordination efforts. Trello enabled seamless communication, task delegation, and collaboration, allowing her to involve her loved ones in the planning process and ensure that every detail was handled with care.

With these AI tools, Anjali was able to manage the complexities of her cultural fusion wedding without losing the essence of what made each tradition so meaningful. They provided her with the support she desperately needed, turning what seemed like an impossible task into a beautifully orchestrated celebration of love and unity.

Key Takeaways: Anjali's Lessons Learned

From her experience, Anjali realized that clear communication and flexibility are essential when planning a multicultural wedding. She learned that coordinating different traditions can be overwhelming, but using AI tools can make the process more manageable. Anjali advises future brides to start planning early and use these tools not just for logistics but also for keeping everyone on the same page, especially when families are spread across different regions. Creating detailed schedules and choosing vendors who have experience with multicultural weddings are key steps. Ultimately, Anjali recommends embracing AI as a valuable resource to help ensure that the wedding day reflects the beauty and significance of both cultures, creating a celebration that everyone can cherish.

Nikeisha's Budget-Friendly Celebration

Background: Planning a Wedding on a Tight Budget

Nikeisha had always imagined a wedding day filled with beauty and joy, but the reality of planning it on a tight budget weighed heavily on her heart. She desperately wanted to create a day that reflected her love and commitment, but the fear of financial limitations casting a shadow over her dream was overwhelming. Every decision felt like a high-stakes gamble, which she was constantly thinking of ways to ensure that her special day didn't lose its magic just because the funds were limited. The pressure to find affordable vendors, manage every penny with care, and still deliver an elegant, unforgettable experience was immense. Nikeisha found herself constantly battling the anxiety that her wedding wouldn't live up to the dream she'd cherished for so long.

How AI Tools Optimized Costs: Budget Tracking and Vendor Selection

When a close friend recommended AI tools to Nikeisha, she was hesitant but willing to give them a shot, hoping they might ease some of her stress. As she began using them, she felt a growing sense of relief and excitement. Finally, she was starting to see her wedding day come together. **Mint**, an AI-driven budgeting app, quickly became her go-to resource, helping her manage every expense and stay on track without feeling overwhelmed. The real time-updates and alerts gave her a newfound sense of control. **Honeyfund** brought unexpected joy as it suggested vendors that fit both her budget and vision, proving that she could have quality without the high costs. **WeddingHappy** provided a detailed checklist and timeline that made her feel organized and empowered, transforming her planning process from stressful to something she genuinely looked forward to. For the first time, Nikeisha felt truly excited, knowing her dream wedding was becoming a beautiful reality.

Key Takeaways: Nikeisha's Tips for Cost-Effective Planning

From her experience, Nikeisha learned several valuable lessons about planning a budget-friendly wedding. Her top advice for future brides includes starting with a clear and realistic budget and using AI tools to track expenses meticulously. She emphasizes the importance of researching and comparing vendors to find the best deals and not being afraid to negotiate prices. Nikeisha also found that prioritizing what mattered most to her and being willing to make compromises on less critical aspects helped her stay within her budget.

The interviews with Makeila, Anjali, and Nikeisha revealed common themes highlighting the transformative power of AI in wedding planning. Each bride faced unique challenges but found AI tools invaluable for organizing, personalizing, and managing their weddings. AI alleviated stress by automating time-consuming tasks, allowing brides to focus on creative and personal aspects.

Overcoming Challenges: Tech Solutions for Common Issues

While AI tools offer numerous benefits, many brides and their families still value traditional wedding planning methods. Balancing modern technology with conventional approaches can be challenging, especially when trying to respect the preferences of older family members or maintain certain cultural traditions.

Challenge One: Tech Savviness

Many brides may feel intimidated by incorporating AI into their wedding planning due to a lack of technical expertise. Overcoming this barrier is crucial to fully leveraging the benefits AI tools offer.

Nikeisha was hesitant to use AI tools for her cultural fusion wedding due to her limited tech skills and tight budget. However, after a friend recommended AI tools, she decided to give them a try. Starting with user-friendly platforms like **Mint**, Nikeisha gradually explored more advanced features as she became comfortable.

Solutions: User-Friendly Interfaces and Support Resources

To address tech savviness, many AI wedding planning tools are designed with user-friendly interfaces. Platforms like **WeddingWire** and **Zola** offer intuitive dashboards and step-by-step guides. They also provide support resources, including tutorials, FAQs, and customer service helplines.

For brides like Nikeisha, starting with basic functions and gradually exploring more complex features can ease the learning curve. Joining online communities where other brides share experiences and tips can provide valuable support. Utilizing demo versions or free trials of AI tools can help brides become familiar with the technology before fully committing.

By focusing on tools with user-friendly designs and using available resources, brides can overcome initial resistance and confidently incorporate AI into their wedding planning. Embracing these technologies can lead to a more organized, efficient, and enjoyable planning experience.

Challenge Two: Balancing AI Tools with Traditional Approaches

Makeila faced the challenge of integrating AI tools with the traditional methods preferred by her family while planning her high-tech fairytale wedding. Her parents and grandparents valued face-to-face vendor meetings and hands-on selection of invitations and decorations. Makeila needed to leverage AI's efficiency while honoring her family's approach.

To balance this, Makeila used AI tools like **WeddingWire** for vendor recommendations and timeline management but made key decisions collaboratively with her family. She identified potential vendors through AI and then scheduled in-person meetings to finalize selections. For invitations and decorations, she gathered ideas online and discussed options with her family during visits to stationery and décor shops. This hybrid method allowed her to benefit from AI's efficiency while involving her family meaningfully.

Solutions: Hybrid Planning Strategies

Combine Online and Offline Research: Use AI tools like The **Knot** and **Zola** for initial research and vendor recommendations. Follow up with in-person visits to finalize choices, blending AI-driven research with traditional interactions.

Incorporate Family Input: Generate options with AI and share shortlists with family members for review and collective decision-making. This ensures family involvement and respect for their opinions while streamlining the process.

Blend Digital and Physical Elements: Utilize AI for budget tracking, guest list management, and timelines. Share these digital elements with involved parties while involving family in selecting physical samples for invitations, décor, and attire.

Educate and Involve Family Members: Teach family members the benefits of AI tools and demonstrate their ease of use. Assign specific tasks that align with their comfort level, like managing the digital guest list or coordinating schedules.

By adopting a hybrid planning strategy, brides can integrate AI tools with traditional approaches, ensuring a balanced wedding planning process that honors both modern efficiency and cherished traditions. This approach maximizes AI's benefits while creating an inclusive and respectful planning experience.

In both cases, AI enhances the wedding planning experience by making it more efficient, organized, and tailored to the couple's unique desires. Whether it's a chic urban celebration or a culturally rich traditional ceremony, AI tools have the versatility to support and elevate the planning process, ensuring that every wedding is a true reflection of the couple's dreams and values.

The Tech Savvy Bride

Laura's Hawaiian Getaway

Planning a destination wedding in Hawaii while living in New York felt like an impossible dream for Laura. The thought of coordinating everything from thousands of miles away was overwhelming, and she often found herself wondering if it would even be possible to create the wedding she envisioned. But then she discovered **Destination Weddings** AI, a comprehensive tool tailored specifically for destination weddings, and everything changed.

With a mix of excitement and relief, Laura dived into the platform, amazed at how it brought Hawaii right into her living room. The tool's virtual reality integration was nothing short of magical, allowing her to step into potential venues, explore them in stunning 3D detail, and feel the ambiance as if she were actually there. Each virtual tour made her dream feel more and more within reach, and the ability to meet with vendors and manage logistics from her home added a sense of control she hadn't thought possible. For the first time, Laura felt a surge of confidence and joy, knowing that her perfect Hawaiian wedding was not just a dream but a beautifully orchestrated reality.

Destination Weddings AI also streamlined communication with local vendors through its built-in translation and timezone synchronization features. Laura could schedule meetings and coordinate with vendors in Hawaii without worrying about time differences or language barriers. The tool's AI-driven scheduling ensured that all parties were kept informed and up to date, making the entire planning process seamless and efficient. Laura's Hawaiian wedding was a stunning success, with every detail perfectly executed, proving that distance is no barrier when you have the right AI tools.

Mia's Italian Countryside Wedding

Mia had always dreamed of a romantic wedding in the enchanting Italian countryside, but the reality of planning it from her home in Canada felt overwhelming. The idea of coordinating every detail from across the ocean left her feeling anxious and uncertain. That was until she stumbled upon **The Knot** platform designed to aid with international weddings. With a mix of hope and excitement, Mia began using the platform, and to her delight, it was as if the tool understood her vision perfectly. **The Knot** presented her with a carefully curated list of vendors and venues that not only fit her style and budget but also captured the essence of the romantic, idyllic setting she had always imagined. The tool's smart matching algorithms took into account her preferences, surprising her with recommendations that exceeded her expectations. For the first time, Mia felt the thrill of her dream wedding coming to life, knowing that even from thousands of miles away, she could create the perfect day in Italy.

One of the standout features of **The Knot** was its ability to handle international regulations and paperwork. The tool guided Mia through the process of obtaining the necessary permits and documents, ensuring that all legal aspects were covered. Additionally, **The Knot** real-time translation feature facilitated smooth communication with Italian vendors, breaking down language barriers and ensuring that Mia's vision was clearly understood. Her wedding in the Italian countryside was everything she had imagined, thanks to the robust capabilities of **The Knot**.

Jordan's Caribbean Escape

Jordan had always imagined an intimate beach wedding on the beautiful island of Jamaica in the Caribbean, with the sound of the waves and a warm breeze setting the perfect scene. But as they started planning, a deep worry began to overshadow their excitement. The thought of managing everything from afar was already daunting, but what really worried them was the fear of choosing a location with a high crime rate. The last thing they wanted was to put their loved ones at risk on their special day.

Alicia Hernandez-Whyle

Desperate for a solution, they discovered **CaribbeanWeddings**, an AI tool designed specifically for Caribbean destination weddings. With a mix of hope and apprehension, Jordan turned to the platform. To their immense relief, **CaribbeanWeddings** did more than just provide virtual venue tours and vendor recommendations; it offered detailed safety information on different locations, guiding them away from areas of concern and helping them find a secure, beautiful spot for their dream wedding. The tool also gave them a comprehensive checklist to stay on top of tasks and deadlines and even included real-time weather forecasts with contingency plans, easing their fears about unpredictable tropical weather.

The most impressive feature of **CaribbeanWeddings** was its ability to create dynamic, adaptable schedules. When a tropical storm threatened to disrupt their wedding plans, the AI tool automatically adjusted the schedule and coordinated with vendors to implement a backup plan. This ensured that Jordan's wedding went ahead smoothly despite the weather challenges. The couple enjoyed a beautiful beach ceremony, confident that **CaribbeanWeddings** had every detail covered.

In summary, the integration of AI in wedding planning has undeniably transformed the industry, providing brides with powerful tools to navigate the complexities of organizing their big day. Through real-life examples of brides like Makeila, Anjali,

Nikeisha, Laura, Mia, and Alex, we see how AI can streamline processes, manage budgets, and incorporate diverse cultural elements, ultimately reducing stress and enhancing the overall experience. These stories highlight the adaptability and effectiveness of AI tools in handling various wedding styles, from high-tech fairytale weddings to multicultural celebrations and budget-friendly events.

Samantha's Success Story: Revolutionizing Wedding Planning with AI

Samantha had been a wedding planner for over a decade, and while she loved her job, she often found herself overwhelmed by the sheer volume of tasks required to pull off a flawless event. Coordinating vendors, managing client expectations, tracking budgets, and ensuring every detail was perfect often left her feeling stretched thin. As her business grew, she knew she needed a better way to manage her workload without compromising on quality or creativity.

That's when Samantha discovered **Wedfuly** AI, an advanced tool designed for wedding planners. At first, she was hesitant after all; she had built her reputation on personal attention to detail and a hands-on approach. But as she began integrating **Wedfuly** AI into her workflow, Samantha was amazed at how it transformed her business.

Alicia Hernandez-Whyle

The AI tool streamlined her vendor management process by offering real-time updates and reminders, ensuring she never missed a deadline. It provided personalized recommendations for venues and services based on her clients' preferences, saving her hours of research and negotiation. Budget tracking became effortless, with the AI generating detailed reports and alerts whenever a budget threshold was approached, allowing her to make informed decisions quickly.

One of the most powerful features was the AI's ability to predict potential issues, such as weather changes or vendor delays, and automatically suggest contingency plans. This proactive approach gave Samantha the peace of mind that no matter what challenges arose, she was prepared.

The real game-changer, however, was how **Wedfuly** AI enhanced her ability to personalize each wedding. By analyzing her clients' tastes, preferences, and feedback, the AI generated unique ideas for themes, décor, and entertainment that resonated deeply with each couple. Samantha could focus more on the creative aspects she loved, knowing that the logistical side was under control.

As a result, Samantha not only delivered exceptional weddings but also expanded her business, taking on more clients without sacrificing the quality of her services. Her clients were thrilled with the seamless, stress-free experience she provided, and word-of-mouth referrals began pouring in.

Samantha's success story is a testament to how AI can revolutionize the wedding planning industry. By embracing technology, she was able to elevate her business, enhance her creativity, and most importantly, provide her clients with the wedding of their dreams.

Whether you're a seasoned planner or just starting out, AI tools like **Wedfuly** can be the key to unlocking new levels of efficiency, creativity, and success in your business.

These success stories illustrate the transformative power of AI in wedding planning, highlighting how technology can overcome even the most daunting challenges. Whether it's managing a budget, blending cultural traditions, or planning a destination wedding from afar, AI tools provide brides with the support they need to turn their dreams into reality. By embracing AI with the right tools at your fingertips, even the most complex weddings can be planned with confidence, creativity, and ease.

Moreover, AI can provide real-time analytics and feedback during the event, allowing hosts to make adjustments as needed. For example, AI can monitor guest engagement and suggest changes to the schedule or activities to keep the event running smoothly. By leveraging AI for efficient event management, hosts can ensure that their events are well organized, enjoyable, and successful.

Final Thoughts

As we come to the end of this journey through the transformative world of AI in wedding planning, it's clear that technology has ushered in a new era of possibilities for brides, grooms, and wedding planners alike. The stories and strategies explored in this book demonstrate how AI can seamlessly blend creativity, personalization, and efficiency, turning the once-daunting task of wedding planning into an enjoyable, manageable, and even exciting process.

From budgeting to venue selection, and from guest management to preserving cherished memories, AI tools have shown their remarkable ability to handle intricate details, streamline processes, and provide innovative solutions to common challenges. These tools not only help in planning a flawless event but also empower couples to infuse their unique personalities into every aspect of their big day, ensuring that their wedding is a true reflection of their love story.

As AI continues to evolve, its role in the wedding industry will undoubtedly grow, offering even more sophisticated and personalized experiences. Whether you are a bride-to-be, a groom, or a professional planner, embracing AI will allow you to stay ahead of the curve, ensuring that your planning process is as smooth and stress-free as possible.

Ultimately, the integration of AI in wedding planning is not just about convenience; it's about enhancing the joy and magic of the journey leading up to one of the most important days of your life. As you step forward into your own wedding planning adventure, may these insights inspire you to leverage the power of AI, helping you create a celebration that is as unforgettable as the love you share.

Alicia Hernandez-Whyle

Appendix

Key Wedding Tasks

Creating a Budget: Establish a budget and track expenses.

Booking the Venue: Select and reserve the wedding and reception venue.

Choosing Floral Arrangements: Select flowers for the ceremony, reception, and bridal party.

Hiring a Photographer: Book a photographer and/or videographer to capture the event.

Arranging Transportation: Organize transportation for guests and the bridal party.

Selecting the Music Playlist: Choose music for the ceremony, cocktail hour, and reception.

Coordinating Catering Services: Plan the menu and organize tastings with the caterer.

Designing Invitations and Save-the-Dates: Choose and send invitations and save-the-date cards.

Planning the Decor: Decide on themes, colors, and overall decor for the venue.

Booking Entertainment: Hire a DJ, band, or other entertainment.

Selecting Attire: Choose the wedding dress, groom's attire, and outfits for the bridal party.

Menu Selection: Finalize the menu with the caterer.

Selecting a Cake: Choose a wedding cake and schedule tastings.

Favors and Gifts: Decide on wedding favors for guests and gifts for the bridal party.

Creating a Timeline: Develop a detailed timeline for the wedding day.

Coordinating with Officiant: Meet with and coordinate the ceremony details with the officiant.

Registering for Gifts: Set up a wedding registry.

Planning the Rehearsal Dinner: Organize the rehearsal dinner the night before the wedding.

Managing RSVPs: Track RSVPs and manage the guest list.

Preparing Speeches and Vows: Write and practice speeches and vows.

Coordinating Hair and Makeup: Book hair and makeup artists for the bridal party.

Planning the Honeymoon: Research and book the honeymoon.

Ensure Legal Requirements: Obtain a marriage license and meet any legal requirements.

List of Vendors Needed

Caterer: Responsible for providing the food and beverages. They ensure that your guests are well fed with delicious meals and drinks.

Photographer: Captures the special moments of your wedding day through stunning photographs. They help preserve the memories of your big day.

Videographer: Records videos of the ceremony and reception, creating a beautiful cinematic experience that you can revisit for years to come.

Florist: Provides floral arrangements and decorations that enhance the beauty of your venue. They help set the mood and theme of your wedding.

DJ/Band: Handles music and entertainment, ensuring your guests have a great time dancing and enjoying the celebration.

Wedding Planner: Assists with overall planning and coordination, helping to bring your vision to life and manage the logistics of the day.

Venue Coordinator: Manages the venue logistics, ensuring everything runs smoothly at the location. They are the point of contact for all venue-related matters.

Officiant: Conducts the wedding ceremony, making it official and personalized to your preferences.

Hair and Makeup Artist: Ensures you and your bridal party look your best with professional hair and makeup services.

Transportation: Provides transport for the bridal party and guests, ensuring everyone arrives on time and in style.

List of categories to consider when budgeting

Venue and Ceremony

Venue rental (ceremony and reception)

Officiant fee

Ceremony site fees

Reception site fees

Decorations (ceremony and reception)

Catering and Food

Catering services

Bar services (alcohol and non-alcoholic beverages)

Wedding cake and/or dessert

Service fees and gratuities

Attire and Accessories:

Wedding dress

Groom's attire (suit, tuxedo)

Accessories (shoes, jewelry, veil, cufflinks)

Hair and makeup

Alterations

Photography and Videography:

Photographer

Videographer

Engagement photo session

Photo albums and prints

Video editing and final product

Entertainment:

DJ or band

Alicia Hernandez-Whyle

Ceremony musicians

Sound system and equipment rental

Dance floor

Flowers and Décor:

Floral arrangements (bouquets, boutonnieres, centerpieces)

Ceremony décor

Reception décor

Lighting

Linens and table settings

Stationery:

Save-the-dates

Invitations

RSVP cards

Programs

Place cards

Thank-you cards

Transportation:

Wedding party transportation

Guest shuttles or parking

Getaway car for the couple

Rings:

Wedding bands for both partners

Ring insurance (optional)

Gifts and Favors:

Wedding favors for guests

Gifts for the wedding party

Gifts for parents

Miscellaneous:

Wedding planner or coordinator

Insurance (wedding insurance)

Legal fees (marriage license, name change)

Tips for vendors

Additional Categories

Accommodations:

Hotel for the couple

Hotel blocks for guests

Bridal suite

Honeymoon:

Travel expenses

Accommodations

Wedding Website:

Hosting fees

Domain registration

Livestreaming:

Services for broadcasting the wedding online

Contingency Fund:

For unexpected expenses (10-15% of total budget)

Wedding Day Timeline Example

Below is an example of a comprehensive wedding day timeline for a ceremony that starts at 4:00 PM. This timeline assumes a traditional wedding format but can be adjusted to fit your specific needs. This timeline can be adjusted based on specific needs, religious customs, or cultural traditions.

7:00 AM – 9:00 AM: Hair and Makeup

- **7:00 AM:** Hair and makeup artists arrive at the getting-ready location (hotel suite, home, etc.).

- **7:15 AM:** Bride starts hair and makeup.

- **7:30 AM:** Bridesmaids and mothers begin hair and makeup rotations.

- **8:00 AM:** Photographer arrives for getting-ready shots (details like the dress, shoes, jewelry, etc.).

- **8:30 AM:** Light breakfast is served for the bridal party.

9:00 AM – 11:00 AM: Groom and Groomsmen Prep

- **9:00 AM:** Groom and groomsmen begin getting ready (shower, shave, dress).

- **9:30 AM:** Photographer moves to the groom's location for getting-ready shots.

- **10:00 AM:** Final touches for the bride's hair and makeup.
- **10:30 AM:** Bride's dress is photographed; bridesmaids help the bride get into her dress.
- **10:45 AM:** Bride's first look with her father or immediate family (if desired).

11:00 AM – 12:00 PM: First Look and Portraits

- **11:00 AM:** First look between the bride and groom (if applicable).
- **11:30 AM:** Couple's portraits around the venue or at a picturesque location nearby.
- **12:00 PM:** Bridal party joins the couple for group photos.

12:00 PM – 2:00 PM: Wedding Party and Family Photos

- **12:00 PM:** Bridal party photos (bride with bridesmaids, groom with groomsmen).
- **12:30 PM:** Family photos with immediate family members (both sides).
- **1:00 PM:** Extended family photos (grandparents, uncles, aunts, cousins, etc.).
- **1:30 PM:** Final couple's photos if needed.

- **2:00 PM:** Everyone heads to the ceremony location.

2:00 PM – 3:30 PM: Final Ceremony Preparations

- **2:00 PM:** Ceremony site setup is finalized (flowers, seating, programs, etc.).

- **2:15 PM:** Final walkthrough at the ceremony site for the couple and wedding party.

- **2:30 PM:** Vendors arrive and set up (musicians, officiant, etc.).

- **3:00 PM:** Guests begin arriving; ushers assist with seating.

- **3:30 PM:** Bride and groom take a few moments to relax and freshen up before the ceremony.

4:00 PM – 4:30 PM: Ceremony

- **4:00 PM:** Ceremony begins with the processional.

- **4:10 PM:** Exchange of vows and rings.

- **4:20 PM:** Pronouncement of marriage, followed by the first kiss.

- **4:25 PM:** Recessional as the newlyweds exit the ceremony space.

- **4:30 PM:** Guests are guided to the cocktail hour.

4:30 PM – 5:30 PM: Cocktail Hour

- **4:30 PM:** Cocktail hour begins; guests enjoy drinks and appetizers.
- **4:45 PM:** Couple and wedding party take a few more photos if needed.
- **5:00 PM:** Couple joins cocktail hour or takes a few private moments.

5:30 PM – 6:00 PM: Reception Setup

- **5:30 PM:** Reception site final touches (table settings, place cards, lighting adjustments).
- **5:45 PM:** Guests are invited to be seated for dinner.
- **6:00 PM:** Bride and groom are announced as they enter the reception.

6:00 PM – 7:30 PM: Dinner and Toasts

- **6:00 PM:** Dinner service begins (plated or buffet).
- **6:45 PM:** Speeches and toasts by the best man, maid of honor, and parents.
- **7:15 PM:** Couple's first dance, followed by parent dances.

7:30 PM – 8:30 PM: Dancing and Cake Cutting

- **7:30 PM:** Open dance floor for guests.
- **8:00 PM:** Cake cutting ceremony.
- **8:15 PM:** Dessert or late-night snacks are served.

8:30 PM – 9:30 PM: Evening Festivities

- **8:30 PM:** Bouquet toss and garter toss (if applicable).
- **8:45 PM:** More dancing and mingling.
- **9:15 PM:** Couple's send-off preparations begin (sparklers, confetti, etc.).

9:30 PM – 10:00 PM: Grand Exit and After-Party

- **9:30 PM:** Grand exit of the bride and groom.
- **9:45 PM:** Guests who wish to continue the celebration head to the after-party location (if planned).
- **10:00 PM:** Vendors begin breakdown and cleanup.

Post-10:00 PM: After-Party (Optional)

- **10:00 PM:** After-party begins at a designated location (hotel lounge, club, etc.).
- **12:00 AM:** After-party winds down.

Alicia Hernandez-Whyle

The Ultimate AI-Powered Wedding Planning Toolkit: Essential Tools for a Seamless Celebration

Comprehensive Wedding Planning Platforms

The Knot: Offers AI-driven tools like a comprehensive wedding planning checklist, personalized vendor recommendations, and a wedding website builder to streamline the entire planning process. *Website:theknot.com*

Zola: Combines wedding registry services with AI-powered planning tools like guest list management and checklist creation. *Website:zola.com*

WeddingWire: Provides AI-powered vendor recommendations, budget planning tools, and customizable wedding websites to help couples organize their wedding efficiently. *Website:weddingwire.com*

Budget Management Tools

Mint: A personal finance tool that can be customized for wedding budgeting, offering AI-driven analysis of spending habits and recommendations on fund allocation. *Website:mint.com*

You Need a Budget (YNAB): Encourages proactive budgeting by using AI to analyze expenses and suggest budget allocations, helping couples stay within their financial limits. *Website:ynab.com*

Honeyfund: An AI-enhanced platform that allows couples to manage wedding and honeymoon expenses by creating funds that guests can contribute to, with real-time budget tracking. *Website:honeyfund.com*

WeddingHappy: AI-driven app for managing wedding budgets, tracking vendor payments, and creating timelines, ensuring all expenses are on track. *Website:weddinghappy.com*

Zola Budget Tool: Provides detailed cost estimates based on wedding size and style, with AI features offering tailored budgeting recommendations and tracking spending in real-time. *Website:zola.com*

Vendor Coordination

WedMatch: Uses AI algorithms to match couples with vendors that fit their style, location, and budget, streamlining the vendor selection process. *Website: wedmatch.com*

HoneyBook: An all-in-one platform that uses AI to manage vendor communications, contracts, and payments, ensuring all logistics are handled smoothly. *Website: honeybook.com*

Aisle Planner: Provides a comprehensive suite of tools for wedding planners, including AI-powered vendor matching and timeline management. *Website: aisleplanner.com*

Appy Couple: Offers AI-powered wedding website creation and guest communication, integrating RSVPs, timelines, and guest lists into one platform. *Website: appycouple.com*

Guest List & Invitations

Joy: An AI-enhanced tool that offers guest list management, RSVP tracking, and digital invitations, all integrated into a personalized wedding website. *Website:withjoy.com*

Paperless Post: Utilizes AI to design and send digital invitations, while tracking RSVPs and managing guest interactions seamlessly. *Website:paperlesspost.com*

Riley & Grey: Provides AI-driven personalized wedding websites and guest communication tools, helping couples manage invitations and RSVPs effectively. *Website:rileyandgrey.com*

RSVPify: AI-powered RSVP management platform that allows for custom RSVP forms, guest list tracking, and real-time updates on guest attendance. *Website:rsvpify.com*

AllSeated: AI-powered platform for creating virtual seating charts and visualizing venue layouts, helping with precise guest placement and venue organization. *Website:allseated.com*

Design & Inspiration

Canva: Offers AI-powered design tools to help couples create wedding invitations, save-the-dates, and other graphics with ease, providing inspiration through customizable templates. *Website:canva.com*

Pinterest Lens: Uses image recognition AI to discover inspiration from photos, aiding in gathering decor and style ideas for weddings. *Website: pinterest.com*

Style Me Pretty: A wedding blog powered by AI that curates personalized inspiration, vendor recommendations, and wedding features based on user preferences. *Website: stylemepretty.com*

ChatGPT: Provides creative wedding planning ideas, advice on various aspects of the wedding, and helps brainstorm unique elements to make the day special. *Website: openai.com/chatgpt*

Claude: An AI assistant that offers personalized suggestions for wedding planning, vendor recommendations and troubleshooting issues. *Website: anthropic.com/claude*

Jasper AI: AI tool that assists with creative tasks, including drafting vendor emails, creating wedding vows, and generating ideas for wedding themes and decor. *Website: jasper.ai*

Venue Selection

Wedding Spot: An AI-powered venue search tool that matches couples with venues based on their budget, style, and guest count. *Website: weddingspot.com*

VenueFinder: Uses AI to provide curated lists of venues that align with a couple's wedding style, location preferences, and budget constraints. *Website: venuefinder.com*

EventUp: An AI-driven platform that offers venue recommendations by analyzing user preferences and providing detailed information on each option. *Website: eventup.com*

Modsy: Offers AI and AR tools for 3D rendering of venues, allowing couples to visualize different decor setups and layouts. *Website: modsy.com*

Google VR Tours: Provides virtual reality tours of potential wedding venues, allowing couples to explore different locations remotely and make informed decisions. *Website: vr.google.com*

Photography & Videography

Flytographer: Connects couples with local photographers around the world using AI to match them with professionals based on style and budget. *Website: flytographer.com*

WedPics: An AI-enhanced photo-sharing app that allows guests to upload and share wedding photos and videos, creating a collaborative album. *Website: wedpics.com*

Shutterfly: Uses AI to suggest photo layouts and designs for wedding albums, prints, and thank-you cards, ensuring a personalized touch. *Website: shutterfly.com*

Pixellu: AI-powered software that automatically designs wedding photo albums by analyzing the best shots and arranging them aesthetically. *Website: pixellu.com*

AI Assistants & Smart Devices

Google Assistant: Can be integrated with wedding planning apps to set reminders, manage appointments, and send quick updates via voice commands. *Website: assistant.google.com*

Alexa: Amazon's AI assistant that can help with hands-free wedding planning by adding tasks to to-do lists, setting reminders, and controlling smart home devices. *Website: amazon.com/alexa*

Siri: Apple's AI assistant that can be used to perform wedding planning tasks, such as scheduling meetings and searching for vendors, via voice commands. *Website: apple.com/siri*

Trello: An AI-enhanced project management tool that can be used to organize wedding tasks, collaborate with the wedding party, and track progress visually. *Website: trello.com*

Asana: AI-powered task management tool that helps couples plan their wedding by delegating tasks, managing deadlines, and tracking progress. *Website: asana.com*

Legal & Administrative

Rocket Lawyer: Provides AI-powered tools for reviewing and generating wedding contracts, ensuring legal compliance and protecting couples from potential issues. *Website: rocketlawyer.com*

LegalZoom: Offers AI-driven contract review and creation services to help couples manage legal documents related to their wedding. *Website: legalzoom.com*

LawGeex: An AI platform that reviews contracts for potential risks, ensuring that wedding agreements are fair and legally sound. *Website: lawgeex.com*

SignNow: AI-powered digital signature tool that allows couples to sign contracts electronically, ensuring secure and legally binding agreements. *Website: signnow.com*

Virtual Reality (VR) & Augmented Reality (AR)

Modsy: Uses AI and AR to create 3D renderings of wedding venues, allowing couples to visualize decor and layout before making decisions. *Website: modsy.com*

Google VR Tours: Offers virtual reality tours of wedding venues, helping couples explore options remotely and make informed choices. *Website: vr.google.com*

Planit Wed: An AR app that overlays digital layouts onto physical spaces, helping couples visualize seating arrangements and decor at their chosen venue. *Website: planitwed.com*

WedSites: Offers AI-powered project management, virtual planning, and budgeting tools, particularly useful for destination weddings or complex events. *Website:wedsites.com*

Accommodation & Travel

Uber: An AI-powered ride-sharing app that helps wedding guests arrange transportation to and from wedding venues, offering convenience and real-time tracking. *Website: uber.com*

Lyft: Another AI-driven ride-sharing platform similar to Uber, which provides transportation options for wedding guests, ensuring everyone arrives on time and safely. *Website: lyft.com*

Airbnb: Provides AI-driven recommendations for wedding guest accommodations, helping them find the perfect place to stay close to the wedding venue. *Website:airbnb.com*

About the Author

Alicia Hernandez-Whyle has devoted her career to helping brides realize their wedding dreams. With more than ten years of experience in the wedding industry, Alicia has guided many couples through one of the most meaningful times in their lives. As both a certified wedding planner and a bridal boutique owner, she truly understands the dreams and aspirations that every bride holds dear.

Alicia's love for weddings goes beyond just organizing an event; it's about turning a bride's dreams into something beautifully tangible and unforgettable. She recognizes the hurdles that come with planning a wedding and has dedicated herself to making the process smoother for everyone involved. From finding that perfect wedding dress to ensuring every detail is just right, Alicia's kindness and expertise shine through in all that she does.

Writing has allowed Alicia to extend her commitment to brides and wedding planners even further. She pours her heart into each page, offering advice and support that feels as reassuring as a trusted friend. Alicia wants every reader to feel understood and supported, knowing they have someone by their side throughout the entire wedding journey.

To Alicia, weddings are not just a job—they're her true passion. Through her work, she hopes to inspire confidence, bring happiness, and create a sense of calm for every bride and planner as they prepare for their big day.

The Tech Savvy Bride

Also By Alicia Hernandez-Whyle

Bridal Bliss: A Guide to Choosing the Perfect Wedding Dress

Journals

Bridal Bliss: Guest List Organizer

Bridal Bliss: Daily Inspirational Log

Bridal Bliss: Vendor Communication Log

Bridal Bliss: Daily Reflection Journal

Bridal Bliss: Daily Wedding Planner and Organizer

Alicia Hernandez-Whyle

www.ingramcontent.com/pod-product-compliance
Lightning Source LLC
LaVergne TN
LVHW021332080526
838202LV00003B/148